Explanation of the practice of 'the *tigle* of the elements'.
Inner fire practice in the mother tantra.

Explanation of the practice of 'the *tigle* of the elements'. Inner fire practice in the mother tantra.

By the Head Teacher of Menri Monastery
Ponlob Tendzin Namdhak Rinpoche

VAJRA
BOOKS

Published & Distributed by

Vajra Books
Jyatha, Thamel, P.O. Box 21779, Kathmandu, Nepal
Tel.: 977-1-4220562, Fax: 977-1-4246536
e-mail: bidur_la@mos.com.np
www.vajrabooks.com.np

First Print, 2019

ISBN 978-9937-9330-8-7

Printed in Nepal

Contents

Foreword by Geshe Gelek Jinpa Rinpoche   vii
Introduction by Florens van Canstein   xi

Part one

The Brief Exposition of the Channels, Winds and *Tigles*   5
     Explanation how pure and impure bodies come
        into existence   7
     Explanation of the channels   13
     Explanation of the winds   37
     Explanation of the *tigles*   67
     Explanation of the letters   75

Part two

Explanation of How to Practice   79
     The methods to control the body   87
     The method to control the mind   105
     Smooth breathing   105
     Medium breathing   115
     Wrathful breathing   117
     Practice with the *tigles*   121
     How to eliminate obstacles   135

Foreword by
Geshe Gelek Jinpa,
abbot of Shenten Dargye Ling

Devotion for the supreme refuge: the spiritual teachers, meditation deities and dakinis.

The Mother Tantra consists of Three Buddha Tantras. It is a great and deep text that is beyond the nine secrets. It is the vehicle of secret mantra of the white A that is the pinnacle of vehicles. It is the heart and life of the ocean of dakinis of the path. It is a text whereby one holds the achievement of Buddhahood in this very life in the palm of one's hand. It is the path left behind by all the victorious ones who have gone to bliss. It is the refined essence of all the collections of the word of the Buddha, precepts and tantras. It is the experience of all great and accomplished knowledge holders. It is the root of all of the mother tantras of secret mantra. It is the state of mind of the empty nature of reality that is good in all respects. It is the crown jewel of the collection of pure tantras.

The primordial teacher Kuntu Zangpo taught this tantra to Kuntu Zangmo and a host of other dakinis. It was transmitted to Zangza Ringtsün in the heaven of thirty-three. Thereafter it appeared in the Sanskrit language. It was transmitted to the practitioner Sangwa Düpa in Olmo Lungring, the country of Shenrab Miwo. It appeared in the language of the teaching in Tagzig. It was transmitted to the practitioner of royal descent Milu Samleg and spread in the Mar language of Zhangzhung. The practitioner Milu Samleg wrote a commentary on the Three Buddha Tantras of Magyu and thus the root text and its commentary came about. Thereafter it was transmitted to the practitioner of inner Zhangzhung Namkha Nangwa Dogcan, the practitioner of middle Zhangzhung Anu Thragthag, and the practitioner of outer Zhangzhung Senegau. The great teacher from Zhangzhung Senegau translated it into Tibetan and thus it came to be spread in Tibet, the land of snow.

During the early spread of the bon teaching this precious teaching was hidden as treasure and later Guru Nontse (born in the Christian year 1136, in a fire dragon year) revealed it in Tanag Dungphor. For a while it remained in two languages[1] but as the Tibetan language prevailed Nyaton Zhonu Bum made a copy and it is said that thereafter this teaching spread widely.

The root text of the Three Buddha Tantras of Mother Tantra and its commentary contain deep key instructions that teach the two stages of tantric practice in a pure unmistaken way. The initiation, transmission and explanation have been transmitted without interruption from the primordial teacher Kuntu Zangpo down to Yongdzin Rinpoche, the master who has the power of speech and who is the holder the treasure of the teaching of the three secrets. Thus their transmission comes to us through the blessing of the great practitioners of the past, like a sweet smell coming from their mouth or like a mist that does not evaporate.

Yongdzin Rinpoche followed in the footsteps of the great practitioners that preceded him. He received initiation, transmission and explanation of the Three Buddha Tantras of Mother Tantra from his main spiritual teacher. He practised the mandala of the King of the Supreme Secret and performed

---

[1] The language of Zhang zhung and Tibetan.

the stages of approaching and realisation in accordance with the tantra. Thereafter he turned the wheel of the teaching and gave initiation, transmission and explanation to his students. Furthermore he also wrote many commentaries. In this way he has become the lineage holder of this teaching in these later times.

Yongdzin Rinpoche has written the 'Practice of the *Tigle* of the Elements' for the benefit of practitioners of both tantra and dzogchen. The translation into English of this text by Florens van Canstein is a work of great merit and benefit. Florens is a direct student of Yongdzin Rinpoche. He has followed Rinpoche and practiced dzogchen for many years. He participated in the meditation school in Shenten Dargye Ling and during its third year, as the programme requires, he practised inner fire for seventy days following 'The Practice of the *Tigle* of the Elements'. On points of doubt he has been able to consult with Yongdzin Rinpoche. That is why I have great confidence in his translation.

Geshe Gelek Jinpa
Shenten Dargye Ling
March 8, 2018

Introduction by
Florens van Canstein

For a practitioner of tantra the practice of 'inner fire' is indispensable. Without it Buddhahood is not possible. Through its practice the practitioner actualizes the pure illusory body and obtains the wisdom of bliss and emptiness. These two are necessary to realize the dharmakaya and rupakaya. For a practitioner of dzogchen it is sufficient to just remain in the natural state to realize Buddhahood. For her the practice of 'inner fire' is a method to enhance the experience of natural state and its practice.

In the Bön tradition the main source for the practice of 'inner fire' or practice with channels, winds, and *tigles,* is the Mother Tantra. In particular the chapter called 'the *tigle* of the elements' and its commentary by Milu Samleg.

For the past eighty years most Bön practitioners have relied on a retreat manual written by Shardza Tashi Gyaltsan when they do intensive practice on inner fire. This retreat manual is part of the 'The Natural Arising of the Three Kayas' and it is mainly, but not exclusively, based on 'the *tigle* of the elements'.

Herein is the translation of a retreat manual on 'inner fire' that is exclusively based on Mother Tantra. The unique characteristic of Mother Tantra is the simultaneous practice of visualisation, breathing and magical movements. 'The *tigle* of the elements' and its commentary by Milu Samleg are rather brief. Therefore, at the request of Geshe Kalsang Gyatso, His Eminence Yongdzin Tendzin Namdhak Rinpoche has written this retreat manual. Yongdzin Rinpoche is the lineage holder of Mother Tantra.

Over a twelve-year period I have been fortunate to receive the extensive initiation into Mother Tantra as well as its complete teaching from Yongdzin Rinpoche. Initially I received the teaching of 'the *tigle* of the elements' in Tibetan from Geshe Kalsang Gyatso who is a Magyu expert, excellent teacher and a long-time friend.

In fall 2016, as part of the meditation school, I participated in a seventy-day 'inner fire' retreat under the inspiring guidance of Khenpo Gelek Jinpa. At that time Yongdzin Rinpoche transmitted 'The *tigle* of the elements' and Khenpo Gelek gave a word-by-word explanation in English. During this time I made a first rough draft translation. After that I consulted with various lamas of whom Geshe Kalsang Gyatso is the main one, to resolve uncertainties. I also consulted Amchi Namse about the many medical terms in the text. Amchi Namse is a Tibetan doctor and Head Teacher of the School Medical for Traditional Medicine at Triten Norbutse Monastery. I would like to express my gratitude to Yongdzin Rinpoche, the above-mentioned lamas and doctor. I also want to thank Khenpo Tenpa Yungdrung who encouraged me while I was making this translation.

I have included the Tibetan text for the benefit of those who know or study the language. Where I think it could be helpful for practitioners I have included a transliteration of the Tibetan.

This book is meant for practitioners who have received transmission of this particular text and intend to do or have done a *tummo* retreat following this retreat manual.

This is the first translation of a text from the collected works of His Eminence Yongdzin Tendzin Namdhak

Rinpoche, the unsurpassed master of Yungdrung Bön of our age. My motivation is to give non-Tibetan students direct access to Rinpoche's writing. My hope is that this will open the door for more capable translators to follow suit and take up the translation of Yongdzin Rinpoche's manifold writings.

I would like to thank Andy Lukianowitz and Colin Millard who have been kind enough to proofread and who have given excellent suggestions.

FLORENS VAN CANSTEIN
Triten Norbutse Monastery
March 20, 2018

Yongdzin Lopön Tendzin Namdak Rinpoche

(Photo: Christophe Moulin)

Sangchog Tharthug Gyalpo
The Main Yidam of Mother Tantra

ཐབས་ལམ་འབྱུང་བའི་ཐིག་ལེའི་ལག་ལེན་བཀང་བ་བཞུགས་སོ། །
འདེགས་ཁྲིད་སྒྲོལ་མའི་ཡུམ་ལ་ཕྱག་འཚལ་ལོ། །

བདེ་བར་གཤེགས་པ་གསང་བ་མཆོག་གི་ལྷ། །
གསང་བ་དགུ་འདུས་ལམ་གྱི་སྒྲུབ་པའི་ཐབས། །
རྩ་རླུང་ཐིག་ལེའི་ཐབས་ཀྱི་འཕྲུལ་འཁོར་ལ། །
བརྟེན་པའི་ལམ་མཆན་མཁའ་འགྲོ་ལ་ཕྱག་འཚལ། །

Explanation of the practice of 'the *tigle*[1] of the elements[2]', the path of method.

Homage to the mother *Degdje Drolma*[3].

Homage to the supreme secret divinity[4], who has gone to bliss,
to the practice method beyond nine secrets[5],
to the magical movements of the method with the channels,
winds and *tigles*,
and to the dakini, guide on whom we rely.

---

1 Tigle (Sanskrit *bindu*) can refer to the natural state, visions or bodily essences. The latter *tigles* are the potential of energy. Physical radiance is their pure aspect. Sperm and ovum are their gross aspect. Given its many and sometimes multi-layered meaning I have chosen to leave the word *tigle* without translation.

2 The Mother Tantra consist of three tantras, each tantra is subdivided in six sections, making eighteen sections in total. In their turn the sections are subdivided in forty-five *tigles*. The commentary by Yongdzin Tendzin Namdak Rinpoche that has been translated here, explains 'the *tigle* of the elements', one of these forty-five *tigles*.

3 Female Liberator who Lifts Up *'degs byed sgrol ma*.

4 King of the Final Supreme Secret (*Sang-chog thar-thug gyal-po*) is the name of the main meditation deity of Mother tantra. The deity represents the natural state.

5 The secret refers to wisdom of awareness itself. This wisdom is beyond the understanding of those following other paths. See 'the *tigle* without degeneration'.

ཐག་མེད་ཡེ་ཤེས་འདོད་འབྱུང་དབྱིག་གི་གཏེར།

།སྒྲུབ་པའི་ལམ་དུ་ཕྱི་ནང་གསང་བ་ཡི།

།འགལ་རྐྱེན་ཞེས་ཚོགས་ཡོངས་སུ་བསལ་བའི་ཕྱིར།

།སྐྱོ་གསུམ་ཐབས་ཀྱི་བྱ་བའི་གཏེར་སྟོ་དབྱེ།

།རིམ་པ་དང་པོས་བསྐྱེད་པའི་ཡི་དམ་སྐུ།

།ཕྱ་མོའི་རྐྱང་སེམས་དཀར་ལ་བསྟིམས་པའི་གཟུགས།

།བདེ་སྟོང་ཡེ་ཤེས་རྡོ་རྗེར་བསྒྱུར་བའི་སྐུ།

།གསང་བདག་རིག་པ་འཛིན་མཆོད་དེ་ལ་བསྟོད།

།ཉི་ཟླ་དཀྱུ་གཅན་དཀག་གི་འབྱུང་འཇུག་བཞིན།

།སྲུང་མཆེད་ཐོབ་པའི་རྐྱང་སེམས་བྱ་བ་ཡི།

།ཆུལ་དང་མཚུངས་པར་བསྒྱིགས་པའི་རྣལ་པ་གང་།

།ཏིང་འཛིན་གསུམ་གྱིས་འབྱུད་པ་རང་ལུགས་གནད།

།སྐུབས་འདིར་སྤྱར་སྣགས་ཀྱི་དོན་འགར་བཀད་པ་རྣམས་ཀྱི་ཡན་ལག་ཏུ་ཙ་ཙུང་ཐིག་ལེའི་ལས་ལ་སྦྱང་བ་བྱེད་པའི་ཆུལ་རང་ལུགས་ཀྱི་རྒྱུད་སྡེའི་དོན་བཞིན་འཆད་པ་ལ།

In order to completely eradicate outer, inner, and secret
adverse conditions and negativities on the path of practice,
I will open the door of the treasure of methodical activities of
the three doors, a wish-fulfilling treasure of pure wisdom.

The first stage is to generate the body of the meditation deity,
this form is dissolved[6] into the purity of subtle wind and mind,
that becomes the deity, whose essence is the wisdom of bliss
and emptiness.
I praise those who perform the activities of knowledge-
holders[7] of the secret lord.

Appearance, increase and obtainment are functions of
wind-mind,
like the occurrence of an eclipse of sun and moon[8].
The key point of our system is that all aspects (of our practice),
that are similar to these functions, are embraced by the three
contemplations[9].

Here as a branch of my earlier explanation of the old tantras[10],
I will explain in accordance with our own tantric cycles[11] how
to practice with channels, winds and *tigles*.

---

6   Dissolve (*bstim pa*) refers to the stage in tantric practice where one
creates the illusory body from the subtle wind and mind in one's heart.

7   There are four types of knowledge holders of inner tantra, practitioners
who have accomplished progressive levels on the path. These four are the
knowledge holders of complete ripening, long life, mudra and spontaneous
presence e.g. The accomplishment of the illusory body is achieved by the
first level of knowledge holder of complete ripening.

8   The eclipse of sun and moon is a poetic description of the meeting of the
original *tigles* of father and mother in the heart during completion stage
practice or during the final stage of the process of dying. At that time we
experience white appearance, red increase, and black obtainment.

9   Unique to inner tantra in bon is that all practice is performed on the
basis of the three contemplations. The three contemplations are the
contemplation of suchness, of compassion and of the seed syllable (i.e. the
visualisation).

10   The writer refers to his earlier commentaries on tantra.

11   i.e. mainly the Mother Tantra Sun of Compassion (*Ma gyu Thug rje
Nyi ma*).

ཚ་རླུང་ཐིག་ལེའི་སྐྱེ་དོན་རྒྱུད་བཞིན་བཀོད་པ་དང་། དེ་དག་ལ་ཁ་ཏུ་ལེན་པའི་ཆུལ་བཀད་པ་དང་གཉིས། དང་པོ་ལ། ཁྲ་སྲུང་གཤིན་རྗེའི་ལས་དག་དང་མ་དག་གི་ལུས་སྒྲུབ་ཆུལ། སྟོང་གཤིན་རྗེའི་དོན་ཉིད་ཐིག་ལེ་ལས་རྩ་བཀད་པ་དང་། སྟོང་གཤིན་རྗེའི་མི་ནུབ་ཐིག་ལེ་ལས་རླུང་བཀད་པ་དང་། སྟོང་གཤིན་རྗེའི་མི་འགྱུར་ཐིག་ལེ་ལས་ཐིག་ལེ་བཀད་པ་དང་། སྟོང་གཤིན་རྗེའི་སྐྱེ་མེད་ཐིག་ལེ་ལས་ཡེ་གི་བཀད་པའོ།

Part one

The brief exposition of the channels, winds and tigles

This text has two parts: a brief exposition of the channels, winds and *tigles* that is in accordance with the tantra, and an explanation how to practice with these.

The first part has five topics:

- The explanation how pure and impure bodies come into existence from 'the *tigle* of the appearing base'[1].
- The explanation of the channels from 'the *tigle* of the nature of existence' from 'the empty base'.
- The explanation of winds from the '*tigle* that does not degenerate' from 'the empty base'.
- The explanation of the *tigles* from 'the unchanging *tigle*' from 'the empty base'.
- The explanation of the letters from 'the unborn *tigle*' from 'the empty base'.

---

[1] The Mother Tantra consists of three tantras. These three are subdivided into eighteen sections. These eighteen are subdivided in forty-five *tigles*. Each of these forty-five *tigles* consists of a sentence of five words. Each *tigle* covers a particular topic and each of the five words relate to a subheading.

།དང་པོ་ནི། །གཞི་ཡེ་སངས་རྒྱས་པའི་རྒྱུད་ལས། །རྗེ་སྡུར་འཆར་ལུགས་ཀུན་རྣམ་པ་ལྔས།
འཆད་དོ། །དང་པོ་རང་འབྱུང་ཡེ་ཤེས་ཆེན་པོའི་རྩལ། །དགའ་བའི་སྐུ་དང་ཞིང་
ཁམས་བསམ་མ་ཁྱབ་ལས། །ཨ་དག་ཕྱགས་རྗེ་ཐབས་ཀྱི་འདུལ་བ་ལ། །སྣང་བ་ཕྱི་
དང་སྙིང་པ་ནང་སྐྱལ་ན་ཏེ། །ཨ་གཡོས་དབྱིངས་ཆེན་ཡེ་ཤེས་ལྷུན་གྱིས་གྲུབ། ། སྐོང་
བཅུད་ཕྱགས་རྗེས་བཟུང་བར་མཛད་པའི་ཕྱིར། །དབྱིངས་ལས་དབྱིངས་བཤན་
ནམ་མཁའ་ཡངས་དོག་མེད། །དེ་ལ་ཡེ་ཤེས་གསལ་བའི་ས་བོན་དུ། །དཀར་སེར་
དམར་ལྗང་མཐོན་ཁ་འབར་བའི་འོད། །རྗ་འཕྱུལ་རྒྱང་གིས་བསྐོང་ཅིང་བསྐོར་བ་
ལས། །ནམ་མཁའ་རྒྱུང་མེ་ཆུ་དང་ས་རྣམས་གྲུབ། །དི་རབ་སྟེང་བཞི་སྟེང་ཕུན་
དཔག་བསམ་དང་། །སྟོང་གསུམ་སྟོང་གི་འཇིག་རྟེན་ཐམས་ཅད་འབྱུང་། །འབྱུང་
བ་ལྷ་ཡེ་དངས་མ་བཅུད་འདུས་པ། །འོད་སྐྱ་ཏི་རྣ་རིན་ཆེན་གོ་འཕྲེང་རྒྱན། །འདི་
ལྟར་སྣང་བ་སྒྱུ་མའི་ཀུན་རྗོབ་ཡར། །

Explanation how pure and impure bodies come into existence

With regard to the first topic, the Tantra of Primordial Buddhahood of the Base says: 'the explanation of the way of arising (of the universe and beings) has five aspects.

First the dynamic energy of self-arising great wisdom manifests inconceivable pure buddha-bodies and buddha-realms, and to liberate impure beings through its compassion it manifests as outer appearance (of the inanimate universe) and inner existence (of animate beings). Without movement they are the spontaneously present wisdom (*yes shes lhun gyis grub*) of the great pure dimension (*dbyings chen*). In order to hold the universe and beings in compassion, pure dimension shows (itself) to pure dimension[2], spacious[3] like the sky. From this (dimension) lights blaze as the seeds[4] of the clarity of wisdom: white, yellow, red, green and blue. A miraculous wind moves and turns about, and thus space, wind, fire, water and earth are created. Mount Meru, the four continents and eight subcontinents, and all the three-thousand-fold universes arise. The pure essence of the elements gathers and opens the door for (the arising of) ornaments like light, sound, sun and moon. In this way the illusion of relative appearance arises.

---

[2] The pure dimension or secret space is emptiness. Thus emptiness arises to emptiness.

[3] The Tibetan *yang dog med pa* literally means neither wide nor narrow.

[4] Seeds (*sa bon*) are the same as the essential purity of the elements (*'byung ba'i dangs ma*).

།རང་འབྱུང་རིག་པའི་ཡེ་ཤེས་དྲི་མེད་དེ། །ཐིག་ལེ་ནང་ལ་འབྱུང་འཕྲག་རྣམ་པ
གསུམ། །དག་པ་དག་བདོ་མ་དག་རིམ་པ་བཞིན། །ཕྱི་གསོག་མགོ་དང་ལུས་ལ
ཞུགས་པའི་ཚེ། །ཨི་གེའི་རྣམ་པ་ལ་དཀར་དུ་དམར་པོ། །འགྲོ་དྲུག་ལས་ཀྱིས་བོན
རིམ་པ་བཞིན། །སྐྱེ་སྦོ་བཞིའི་ཡི་རྟེན་ལ་བབས་མ་ཐག །ཕུན་སྐྱེས་སྐྱས་སྐྱབས་ཆོད་ཀྱི
རྟེན་ལ་བརྟེན། །མཉམ་ཆོང་བདུད་རྦྱུད་ལས་ཀྱི་རྐུང་གིས་གཡོས། །འཐབ་པའི
སྦོངས་ཀྱིས་འོད་ལས་རེར་དུ་འཕྲོས། །ཤེམས་ལས་ཡིད་སྤྱུལ་ཀུན་བཟང་ཡབ་ཡུམ
གཉིས། །ཁ་མའི་སྤ་ལ་བབས་ནས་ལས་ཀྱིས་འཕུད།

There are three ways in which this stainless self-arising wisdom awareness enters animate existence: in a pure, partially pure[5], or impure way. When it enters the crown of the head or (elsewhere in) the body it takes the form of a white A or red HA. In accordance with the karma of the six types of sentient beings[6] (self-arising wisdom) descends into a body of one of the four types of birth. Immediately and simultaneously, moved by the karmic wind, a deity with a light body and a demon appear. Due to strength of (their) strife[7] rays radiate from the light. From the mind[8] (*sems*) manifests energy[9] (*yid*) that descends into the regenerative fluids of father and mother, Samantabadra and Samantabadri in union, where it meets its karma.

---

5   Partially pure refers to bodhisattvas who have purified the obscurations of the disturbing emotions but still need to purify the obscurations to omniscience.

6   It is explained how through the force of karma impure sentient beings take birth but not how pure and partially pure beings take birth.

7   The strife between the deity and the demon represents the strife between positive and negative karma or between knowledge and ignorance.

8   The mind that is about to take birth.

9   Here *yid* refers to the subtle energy or karmic wind that supports consciousness. It is part of the triad karmic imprints, energy and mind (*bla yid sems gsum*).

ཀྱུང་དེ་ལས། སྲ་དགུ་དོ་བཅུ་སྐྱེས་ནས་རྣ་གསུམ་པར། །ཡེ་ཤེས་ནི་ལྟ་དེ་ལྟར་རྟོགས་
ཆུལ་སྟོན། །དེ་དུས་ཡེ་ཤེས་ཐིག་ལེ་རེ་ལྟར་ན། །ཡེ་ཤེས་ཆུབ་དང་འགགས་པ་དོན་ལ་
མེད། །ཀུན་རྟོབ་རང་སྲང་དབང་གིས་འགྲིབ་ན་ཡང་། །ཡེ་ཤེས་མཐུ་ལས་དབུས་
མཐིང་བསམ་གཏན་རྒྱ། །ཡར་སྟེ་ཆངས་ཐུབ་མར་སྟེ་གསལ་བར་རྫུ། །ཨང་ས་རྒྱལ་
གྱིན་འཕགས་སེམས་དཔའ་བརྗེས་པའི་ཆུལ། །རིང་ཐུང་ཆེ་ལ་ཕྲ་སྦོམ་བསོད་
ནས་ཏེ། །ཡང་དོག་ཡེ་ཤེས་དང་འཁྲིག་བཟང་དན་སྟོན། །ཁྱལས་དཀར་གཡོན་
དམར་དཔུས་ལ་འཁྲིལ་ནས་ཡོད། །མར་སྟེ་སྟེ་ཕོག་ཡར་སྟེ་སྲ་སྟོར་དོད། །དེ་ལས་
གྱིས་པའི་འཁོར་ལོ་སླ་པོ་རེ། །ཞེས་སོ།

།གཞུང་འདིས་གཞི་ཡེ་ཤེས་ཐིག་ལེ་ལས་སྟོང་བཅུད་རེ་ལྟར་ཤར་ཆུལ་དང་། ནང་
བཅུད་ཀྱི་འགྲོ་བ་དག་དང་མ་དག་པའི་སྐྱེ་གནས་བཟུང་ཆུལ་དང་། དེ་ལྟར་སྐྱེ་
གནས་བཟུང་བའི་དུས་སུ་ཡེ་ཤེས་ཀྱི་རང་བཞིན་རེ་ལྟར་གནས་པ་སོགས་བསྟན།

The tantra says: 'During the first three months of the nine months and ten days after conception, the forty-five wisdom (*tigles*) seem to be exhausted. How do the wisdom *tigles* abide during this period? In reality wisdom has not disappeared or ceased. Though it is obscured by the self-appearance of the relative, from its power the blue central channel of mental stability[10] reaches upward to the crown and downward to the secret place. Going upward for buddhas it protrudes outwards, but for bodhisattvas it does not[11]. Its length is like the thumb's phalange, its width depends on merit, its openness on wisdom, and its straightness on good and bad (karma). The white right channel and the red left channel touch[12] the central channel. Their lower ends reach below the navel and the higher ends reach the nostrils, and from these the five chakras branch out[13].'

This (the above) text explains how from the base, which is the wisdom *tigle*, the world and its inhabitants arise, how beings take pure and impure birth, and how the nature of wisdom abides when they take birth.

---

[10] The central channel is called the channel of mental stability because inside it the rough winds of the disturbing emotions do not move.

[11] Buddhas have a crown protrusion, bodhisattvas don't.

[12] Literally it says the lateral channels coil around the central channel. Khenpo Gelek comments that actually they only touch the central channel at the chakras.

[13] The chakras branch out at the places where the lateral channels touch the central channel.

གཞིས་པ་བོན་ཉིད་ཐིག་ཐིག་ལེའི་འགྲེལ་པ་ལས་རྩ་ཡི་རྣམ་བཤད་བཀོད་པ་ནི། ཡང་
དག་པར་རྩ་ཡོ་ན་བསྙེན་པ་ནི། ཌ་ར་བོ་སྲུ་གུ་དང་བཅས་པར་ཁྲག་རྒྱུ་སྤྲུང་རྒྱུ་བ་ལ།
ཌེས་ཚིག་ལུས་དང་དབང་པོ་སྲོག་ཌོན་སྟེང་ཐབས་ཙད་ཀྱི་རྩ་བར་གྱུར་པས་ན་རྩ་
ཞེས་བྱའོ། །ཡང་ན་སྐྱེ་གནས་འཕོས་འགྲོབ་འཆི་བ་ལེ་ཤེས་སྐྱེ་བའི་རྩ་བ་ཡིན་པས་
ན་རྩ་ཞེས་བྱའོ། །རྒྱུ་ནི་འབྱུང་ལྔའི་ཕུང་པོའི་སྟེང་ལས་རྩ་ཐམས་ཅད་འབྱུང་བ་
ཡིན་ཏེ། ས་བོན་ལས་སྐྱུ་གུ་སྐྱེ་བ་བཞིན་ནོ།

Explanation of the channels

As to the second topic: the exposition of the channels (is given in) the commentary[14] on 'the *tigle* of the nature of reality'. Just to explain the word channel correctly:

- The essence of the channels is that they are hollow: blood, moisture and wind move through them.
- The etymological definition is that channels (*rtsa*) are called 'roots'[15] because they are the foundation of the body, sense faculties, life, and the essential organs. They are also called 'roots' because they are the foundation or root of conception, growth, decline, death and the generation of wisdom.
- Concerning their cause: in the way that sprouts come forth from seeds, all the channels come forth from physical heart made up of five the elements.

---

[14] The commentary by Milu Samleg.
[15] The Tibetan word for channel *rtsa* literally means root.

།དབྱེ་བ་བཤད་གཞུང་མང་ཡང་། ཐེག་པ་ཆེན་པོ་གསང་སྔགས་མ་རྒྱུད་འདིའི་
དགོངས་པ་ལ་ལྟ་སྟེ། །ཨེ་ཤེས་རྒྱུ་བའི་རྩ་སྟ། དོད་རྒྱུ་བའི་རྩ་སྟ། རླུང་རྒྱུ་བའི་རྩ་སྟ།
ཁྲག་རྒྱུ་བའི་རྩ་སྟ། ཐེག་ལྗེའི་དྭངས་མ་རྒྱུ་བའི་རྩ་སྟ། དེ་ལས་གྲྱེས་པའི་རྩ་བརྒྱ་
དང་རྩ་བརྒྱད། དེ་ལས་ཕྱི་ནང་བར་གསུམ་གྱི་མཚོན་རྩ་སྲུམ་བདུན་དུག་སྟ། དེ་ལས་
མགོ་དང་ཡན་ལག་གི་རྩ་ཆེན་བདུན་བརྒྱ་དེ་ག །དེ་ལས་རྩུང་མཐིས་བད་གར་
འདུ་བའི་རྩ་བརྒྱུད་ཁྲི་བཞི་སྟོང་། དེ་ལས་ཕྱ་མོའི་རྩ་ཕྲན་བདུན་འབུམ་ཉི་ཁྲི་གྲྱེས་
པ་ཡིན་ཏེ།

Concerning their categories many texts give (different) presentations but according to the Mother Tantra of secret mantra, the great vehicle that we follow here, there are five categories:

- Five channels through which wisdom moves;
- Five channels through which light moves;
- Five channels through which winds move;
- Five channels through which blood moves; and
- Five channels through which the pure essence of the *tigles* move.

From these hundred and eight channels branch out, and from these three hundred and sixty outer, inner and middle channels[16]. From these seven hundred and twenty major channels connected to the head and limbs. From these eighty-four thousand channels through which flow bile, wind, phlegm and their combination. From these seven hundred and twenty-thousand subtle minor channels.

---

[16] Because all of them come forth from the life (force) channel here they are called *mtshon rtsa* which is another name for the life (force) channel (*srog rtsa*).

དེ་ལྟ་བུའི་དགོས་པ་ཡང་། །རྒྱུད་འདི་ཉིད་ལས། །རྒྱ་བ་གཅིག་ལ་ཡེ་ཤེས་སྟོང་པོ་
གསུམ། །འབྱོར་ལོ་ལྷ་ལ་ཡེ་ཤེས་ཞེ་ལྷ་གནས། །བྱི་རྩར་ཁྲག་རྒྱུ་ནང་རྩར་སྨག་ས་མ་
རྒྱུ། །གསང་རྩར་རླུང་རྒྱུ་རྩ་ཆེན་བརྒྱ་རྩ་བརྒྱད། །རྩ་ཕྲན་སུམ་བརྒྱ་བརྒྱད་ཁྲི་བཞི།
སྟོང་གྱེས། །གཡོགགས་ནས་ཡེ་ཤེས་རྩ་རྣམས་ཐྲལ་པ་ཡི། ཞེས་བཤད་པའི་དོན་ནོ།

།དེ་ལས་རྩ་བ་གཅིག་ཅེས་པ་ནི། སྟིང་གི་དཀྱིལ་ན་རྩ་ཡི་རྒྱལ་པོ་ཤེས་གང་ག་རེ་
འདུག །རེང་ནང་ཕྱུང་ཚོན་གང་ག་ཕྱུ་སྐོམ་ཏེ་ར་ར་བཅུ་ཚལ་ཚམ། གསོ་བ་རེག་པས་ཡང་
རྗེ་དཀར་པོ་བཏགས། །གསང་སྐྱགས་པའི་ཡེ་ཤེས་གཏུག་མའི་རྩར་བཏགས། རང་
འབྱུང་རིག་པའི་རྟེན། །གསང་མཆོག་མཐར་ཐུག་གི་ཌོ་རྗེར་ཡོད། དེ་ལ་ཡང་སྟོང་པོ་
གསུམ་ནི། །གཡས་དཀར་གཡོན་དམར་དབུས་མཐིང་སྟོང་གསས། །བདེ་བའི་རྩ་ཡོད་
པ་དེ་གསུམ་གསུམ་དུ་བསྒྲགས་པ་དང་།

The same tantra also explains what we need for practice: 'One channel has three wisdom trunks. In the five chakras abide forty-five wisdoms. There are one hundred and eight major channels: blood moves in the outer channels, both blood and wind[17] move in the inner channels, and wind moves in the secret channels. From these three hundred sixty[18] up to eighty-four thousand minor channels branch out that by pressing upon it close the wisdom channel.'

What is called the 'one channel' in this quotation is the king of channels. It is like a white crystal in the centre of the heart[19]. Its length is as that of the phalange of the thumb. Its thickness is as ten hairs of a horse's tail. In medicine it is called 'the white overlord' (*yang rje dkar po*). In tantra it is called 'the channel of natural authentic wisdom' (*ye she nug ma'i rtsa*). It is the support of self-arising wisdom. It is present as the essence *Sangchog Thartug*[20]. This (channel) has three trunks: white on the right, red on the left and blue in the centre. The trunks have (the qualities of) emptiness, clarity and bliss[21]. So these are known as three.

---

[17] Literally *sbag ma* means layered.

[18] The text says three hundred, which is short for three hundred and sixty.

[19] In dzogchen texts this channel is called the *kati* channel.

[20] *Sangchog Tharthug* is the main yidam of mother tantra. His essence is primordial wisdom.

[21] If one practices with these trunks (channels) the experiences of emptiness, clarity and bliss will arise.

སྟེང་གི་རྩ་དེ་ལས་ལྡོན་པོའི་རྩ་བཞི་གྱེས་པ་དེ། ཐིག་ལེའི་དྭངས་མ་རྒྱའི་ཐིགས་
ཕྲན་ལྟ་བུ་རྒྱུ་བའི་རྒྱ། སྲིད་པ་གཞི་འཛིན་ཞེས་བྱ་བ། དབང་གི་རྩ་མོ་གནས་དགར་
མའི་ངོ་བོར་ཡོད་དོ། །མདངས་སམ་འོད་ཀྱི་དྭངས་མ་ཁ་དོག་སྣ་ཚོགས་སུ་གསལ་
བ། གཞན་ཚོན་ལྟ་བུའི་རྩ་དབང་པོ་གསལ་བྱེད་ཅེས་བྱ་བ་དང་། དབུགས་ཀྱི་
དྭངས་མ་ས་ལེ་སྦྲམས་འོག་ཏུ་བཅུག་པའི་རྣངས་པ་ལྟ་བུའི་རྩ། འཁོར་ལོ་སྒྱུར་
བྱེད་ཅེས་བྱ་བ་དང་། ཁྲག་གི་དྭངས་མ་མཚལ་ཚོག་ལ་ཕྱུར་བའི་ཟེར་ལྟ་བུའི་རྩ།
གསལ་བྱེད་མདངས་འབྱིན་ཞེས་བྱ་བ་དང་། རྩ་དེ་རྣམས་སངས་རྒྱས་ཡུམ་བཞིའི་
ངོ་བོར་དག་པ་དན་པའོ། །དག་པའི་རྩ་ལྟ་པོ་དེ་ལ་ཡེ་ཤེས་ཀྱི་ཐིག་ལེ་རྒྱ་ཁབའི་ཟིལ་
པ་ལྟ་བུ། འབོ་ལ་ཁད་པ་འབོ་ནི་མི་འབོ་བར་གནས་སོ། །སྤྱི་པོ་བདེ་ཆེན་འཁོར་ལོ་
ལྟ་གཅིག་ཏུ་སྟེ། དྭངས་མའི་རྩ་ལྟ་གཅིག་ཏུ་སྟེ། སྟོང་པོ་རྣམ་པ་གསུམ་དང་དེ་
རྣམས་ནི་ཡེ་ཤེས་རྒྱ་བའི་རྩ་ལྟ་ཞེས་བྱའོ།

From the channel in the heart four minister channels branch out:

- The channel in which the pure essence of *tigles* moves, like small drops of water, is called 'the channel that holds the base of existence'. It has the essence of 'the White Powerful Goddess of the White Place' (*dbang gi lha mo gnas dkar ma*)[22];
- The channel in which the pure essence of radiance or light is clear as various colours, like a rainbow, is called 'the channel that makes the sense faculties clear';
- The channel (in which) the pure essence of breath (moves), like the vapour of fine gold buried under the ground, is called 'the channel that turns the wheel';
- The channel (in which) the pure essence of blood (moves), like rays coming forth from cinnabar, is called 'the channel that makes clear and exudes radiance'.

These four channels are considered to be pure. In essence they are the Four Mother Buddhas[23]. On (top of) these pure channels wisdom *tigles* abide in the way that dewdrops abide on a stalk of grass, about to spill over. When we consider the five chakras such as the crown chakra etc. as one 'channel', and the five channels (where) the pure essences (move) as one 'channel', than together with the three trunks, they are called the five channels where wisdom moves[24].

---

22 A female deity in the Magyu mandala.
23 The Four Mother Buddhas are four deities in the Magyu mandala.
24 By practising with these wisdom channels wisdom arises.

།དེ་ནས་འོད་རྒྱ་བའི་ཚ་ལུ་ནི། སྙིང་གི་དབང་པོ་གསལ་བྱེད་ལས་ཀྱིས་ནས་ཡོད་དོ། །འཇུག་པའི་ཚོགས་དྲུག་འོད་དང་ཟེར། །དཀར་འཇམ་བོག་པ་སྟོང་བའི་རྒྱ། །ས་ལེ་སློན་མ་འོད་དཀར་རྒྱ། །ཏུག་ཏུ་མིག་ལ་འོད་འབྱོར་འབྱིལ། །ཤུང་འཇམ་བོག་པ་སྟོང་བའི་རྒྱ། གསུ་བུན་རྒྱུ་གི་འོད་ལྡང་ཁ། །ཏུག་ཏུ་སྙ་ལ་དེ་བསྟན་འབྱུང་། །དམར་འཇམ་བོག་པ་སྟོང་བའི་རྒྱ། །བདུད་རྩི་གྲོལ་བའི་འོད་དམར་རྒྱ། །ཏུག་ཏུ་སྦྱེ་ཡིས་མཚོན་བྱང་སྐྱོང་། །སྨྲོ་འཇམ་བོག་པ་སྟོང་བའི་རྒྱ། །འཕུལ་གྱི་སྐྱ་འཇིན་འོད་སྟོན་རྒྱུ། །ཏུག་ཏུ་རྣ་བར་ང་སྐྱ་འབྱུང་། །སེར་འཇམ་བོག་པ་སྟོང་བའི་རྒྱ། བྱིན་ཆེན་སྐྱུན་པོའི་འོད་སེར་རྒྱུ། །ཏུག་ཏུ་ལུས་ལ་བདེ་བ་འཆར། །གཞན་ཚོན་སྣ་ལྔ་རྒྱ་བའི་རྒྱ། ཕྱག་ལེ་བྲག་གིས་མ་གོས་པ། མཉེན་འཇམ་དབང་པོ་སྟོ་ལྷར་ཐུང་ལུས་ནི་འཇིག་ལ་ཉེ་བ་ན། །ལྷ་པོ་བརྒྱགས་ནས་སྙིང་ལ་འདུས། །ཞིས་བྱ་བ། ལྷ་པོ་དེ་ཕ་མཉེན་འཇམ་པོ་འོད་ལྔ་རྒྱ་བའི་ཚུ་འོ།

།ཁྲུ་རྒྱ་བའི་ཚ་ལུ་ནི། སྙིང་གི་འབྱོར་བོ་སྐྲ་བྱེད་ལས་ཀྱིས་ནས་ཡོད་དེ། གོང་དུ་བསྟན་པའི་དོན་སྙིང་ལྷ་ནས་བཀྱུད་དེ་མགོ་དང་ཞབ་ལཀ་ཞི་ལས་ཀྱིས་པའི་ཚ་ཆེན་ཕྱོ།

There are five channels in which light moves that branch out from (the minister channel in the) heart 'that makes the senses clear'. The six engaging aggregates (six consciousness) are (like) light and rays:

- White light that is like a clear lamp moves in the smooth white channel that is empty inside. Continuously the wheel of light turns in the eyes;
- Green light that is like a wisp of fog moves in the smooth green channel that is empty inside. Pleasant smells arise continuously to the nose;
- Red light that is like liberating nectar moves in the smooth red channel that is empty inside. Continuously the tongue tastes enlightenment;
- Blue light that is like the beholder of magical sound moves in the smooth blue channel that is empty inside. Continuously roaring sound appear to the ears;
- Yellow light that is like a mass, a great gift[25], moves in the smooth yellow channel that is empty inside. Continuously bliss arises in the body.

In these five channels that are pliant and smooth, light moves like rainbows, not covered by *tigles* or blood, and reaches the sense organs. When the body is approaching destruction (death) these five (lights) return to and dissolve in the heart.' These are five pliant and smooth subtle channels where light moves.

The five channels in which winds move, branch out from 'the minister channel that turns the wheel' in the heart. They connect to the abovementioned five essential organs and branch out further into the head and the four limbs.

---

[25] The term 'a great gift' is poetic term for the body.

།ཁག་རྒྱུ་བའི་རྩ་ལྟ་ནི། །སྙིང་གི་གསལ་བྱེད་མདངས་འཕྲིན་ལས་ཀྱེས་ནས་ཡོད་དེ། །སྙིང་སྐྱེད་པ་སྲུམ་སྐྱིལ་མ། །སྐྲོ་བ་སྐྱེད་པ་དྲི་ཟ་བྲལ་མ། །མཆིན་པ་སྐྱེད་པ་དགུ་རྩེ་མ། །མཁལ་མ་སྐྱེད་པ་རགས་སྡོམ་མ། །མཆེར་པ་སྐྱེད་པ་སྒྱུ་མ་དང་ལྷ་ཡད། །གོང་བཞིན་དོན་ལྔ་ནས་ཡན་ལག་མགོ་ལྔ་ནས་ཀྱེས་ཏེ་གཏེ་བ་མདངས་ཁྲག་རྒྱུའོ།

The five channels in which blood flows branch out from the minister channel in the heart 'that makes clear and exudes radiance':

- The channel that develops the heart is (called) 'three intertwined'[26];
- The channel that develops the lungs is (called) 'without smell';
- The channel that develops the liver is (called) 'nine peaked'[27];
- The channel that develops the kidneys is (called) 'thick and rough'; and
- The channel that develops the spleen is (called) '(empty like) bamboo'.

As above they branch out to the five essential organs and from there to the limbs and head. Blood moves in them giving a radiant complexion.

---

[26] Energy and blood flow respectively through a white channel and a black channel that are intertwined. There is an explanation of three channels in the heart in the *yas ru a khri chenmo*.

[27] This channel supports digestion.

ཁྱིག་ལེ་རྒྱུ་བའི་རྩ་ལྟ་ནི། སྲིང་གི་རྩ་སྦྲིད་པའི་གཞི་འཛིན་ནས་ཀྱིས་ནས། སྐྱེད་སྲད་
བར་དུ་གྱིས་ཏེ། རྩ་གཞིག་ལྟེ་བའི་ཨེ་ལ་ཟུག་སྟེ་སྲིད་པ་ཆགས་པའི་རྟེན་གཞི་བྱེད་
དོ། །རྩ་གཞིག་ཕྱགས་པའི་ཨ་ལ་ཟུག་སྟེ་དྲུན་པ་གསལ་བའི་སྐྲོན་མ་བྱེད་དོ། །རྩ་
གཞིག་མགྲིན་པའི་ཨྃ་ལ་ཟུག་སྟེ་གསུང་དབྱངས་སྐྲོག་པའི་ང་རོ་འབྱིན་ནོ། །རྩ་
གཞིག་སྙི་བོའི་ཧྃ་ལ་ཟུག་སྟེ་བྱང་ཆུབ་ཐོབ་པའི་ལམ་དུ་བྱེད་དོ། །རྩ་གཞིག་གསང་
བའི་བྃ་ལ་ཟུག་སྟེ་ས་བོན་རྒྱ་བའི་ལས་བྱེད་དོ། །དེ་ལྟ་ནི་རྩ་མདུད་ཐིག་ལེའི་རྟེན་
ཡི་གེའི་གཟུགས་ཅན་དུ་ཡོད་དེ་རྒྱས་པ་ཐིག་ལེའི་འཁྱིལ་བར་གོ་ཕྱག་ཡི་ཤེས།

From the ministerial channel 'that holds the base of existence' at the heart five channels, in which the *tigles* move, branch out upward, downward and horizontal:

- One channel reaches the E at the navel (chakra), it is the basic support for coming into existence[28];
- One channel reaches the A at the heart (chakra), it is the lamp that makes the mind clear;
- One channel reaches the OM at the throat (chakra), it issues forth the reverberating roar of melodious speech;
- One channel reaches the HUM at the crown (chakra), it is the path for obtainment of enlightenment[29]; and
- One channel reaches the BAM in the secret (chakra), it makes the seed move.

These five channels have knots in the form of letters that support *tigles*. One will obtain deep understanding (by reading) the extensive commentary on the *tigle*[30].

---

[28] In Tibetan medicine the body is considered to grow from the navel and therefore this channel is considered to be the first.

[29] In dzogchen the path for obtainment of enlightenment is the *kati* channel.

[30] i.e. the commentary on 'the unborn *tigle*'.

དེ་ལས་གྲུབ་པའི་རྩ་ཆེན་བརྒྱ་དང་རྩ་བཅུད་ནི། རླུང་པ་དར་གྱི་དཔྱང་ཐག་སུམ་
ཅུ་རྩ་གཉིས། བྱང་ལོག་འཕུལ་གྱི་མདོ་འཛིན་སུམ་ཅུ་རྩ་གཉིས། ཡན་ལག་གྱུར་གྱི་
འཐེབ་ཐག་སུམ་ཅུ་རྩ་གཉིས། གཞུངས་པ་རྩ་ཡི་རྒྱལ་པོ། སྦོག་རྩ་རྩ་ཡི་རྒྱལ་མོ་
གཉིས། དེ་ལས་གྲུབ་པ་སྨས་པའི་རྩ་དྲུག །ཚངས་པའི་སྐུད་པ། དར་གྱི་དཔྱང་ཐག
གཉན་གྱི་རེ་ཐག སྤོག་གི་འགྱིང་ཐག མཆེན་པའི་རྩ་སྟོང་། མཁལ་མའི་རྩ་ནག་པོ
།མཛིན་དུ་གྱུར་པའི་རྩ་དྲུག་གོ །ཡལ་ལག་གི་ལྟ་རྩ་ཆེན་པོ་བཞི། དཔྱལ་བའི་གསེར་
མདོངས། ཕྲག་པའི་སྒྱུལ་མིག་འཕོར་མོ། དེ་ལྟར་དཔྱང་ཐག་རྩ་དཀར་ཡིན་པས་
ནང་རྒྱུང་རྒྱུ། མདོ་འཛིན་འཁྱག་མེད་ཡིན་པས་འདྲེས་མ་རྒྱུ ཡན་ལག་གཡོ་བསྐྱོད་
ཡིན་པས་ཕྱི་རྩར་ཁྲག་རྒྱུ་བ་དང་རྩ་ཐབ་བརྒྱ་དང་རྩ་བཅུད་དོ།

From these hundred and eight major channels branch out:

- Thirty-two channels in the brain that are like silk cords hang that down;
- Thirty-two channels of magical manifestation in the chest that come from one point[31];
- Thirty-two channels in the limbs that are like tent ropes;
- The two: the king of channels is the spinal cord and the queen of channels is the life channel;
- From these (abovementioned two) branch out six channels that are hidden[32] and six discernible channels which are: 'the thread at the crown', 'the silk hanging cord', 'the strong yak-hair ropes'[33], 'the long cord of life', 'the blue channel in the liver' and 'the black channel in the kidneys'; and
- Four major visible channels[34] of the limbs: 'the golden peacock's eye' on the forehead and 'the round snake's eye' at the back of the neck'. The channels that hang down like (silk) cords are white, wind moves inside of them. The channels that come from one point are faultless, a mix (of wind and blood) moves inside of them. Blood flows in the external channels that allow movement of the limbs.

These are the hundred and major eight channels.

---

[31] *mdo 'dzin* is the central bead on a mala. 'That come from one point (*mdo 'dzin*)' means that these channels spread out from a single point.

[32] These six hidden channels are not included in the count of hundred and eight major channels.

[33] The medical tantras.present a clear explanation of the channels, winds and *thigles*. e.g. 'the strong yak hair rope' (*mnyan gyi re thag*) are four channels that come down from the pulsating channel at the top of the head, two to the neck and two to the throat.

[34] *lta rtsa* are visible channels in the sense of perceptible.

།དེ་ལས་གྲེས་པའི་ཕྱུམ་བཅུ་དྲུག་ཅུ་འི། ཕྱི་གདགས་ས་ཕྱིབ་ཀྱི་མཚོན་ཆ་བཅུ་ཉེ་ཤུ། བར་ཚུས་པའི་འཇེན་ཆ་བཅུ་ཉེ་ཤུ། གསང་བ་དོན་སྐྱིང་གི་གཟུངས་ཆ་བཅུ་ཉེ་ཤུ།

དེ་ལས་གྲེས་པའི་བདུན་བཅུ་ཉེ་ཤུ་འི། མགོ་བོ་དང་ཐབག་གྱུར་ཉིང་འདང་བ་བཅུ་བཅུད་ཅུ། ཞང་ལོག་སྐྲ་འཕུལ་དུ་བ་འདང་བ་བཅུ་བཅུད་ཅུ། རོ་སྐྲད་གཡུང་དུང་ཐིག་སྐོར་འདང་བ་བཅུ་བཅུད་ཅུ། ཡན་ལག་སྱིད་པའི་གཉེན་ལས་འདང་བ་བཅུ་བཅུད་ཅུ། དེ་ལྟར་བདུན་བཅུ་ཉེ་ཤུའོ།

།དེ་ལས་གྲེས་པ་རྐྱང་གི་འཕར་ཆ་ཉེ་ཉི་བྲི་ཆེག་སྐོང་། མཐིས་པའི་དོང་ཆ་ཉེ་ཉི་བྲི་ཆེག་སྐོང་། བད་ཀན་ཉིན་ཆ་ཉེ་ཉི་བྲི་ཆེག་སྐོང་། ཁྲག་གི་རྒྱ་ཆ་ཉེ་ཉི་བྲི་ཆེག་སྐོང་། དེ་ལྟར་བཅུད་བྲི་བཞི་སྐོང་རོ།

From these three hundred and sixty channels branch out:

- Hundred twenty external[35] perceptible channels move up and down[36];
- Hundred twenty middle channels that go along the bones;
- Hundred twenty secret channels (that foster) health of the essential organs.

From these seven hundred and twenty channels branch out:

- Hundred and eighty in the head like cords (attached to a) tent's wooden pole;
- Hundred and eighty in the chest like a miraculous net;
- Hundred and eighty in the lower part of the body like a carpenter's swastika ruler; and
- Hundred and eighty in the limbs that are like pliable paths of existence:

From these eighty-four thousand channels branch out:

- Twenty-one thousand channels through which pulsates wind;
- Twenty-one thousand channels through which flows the warmth of bile;
- Twenty-one thousand channels through which flows cohesive phlegm;
- Twenty-one thousand channels through which moves blood.

---

[35] In this paragraph external, middle and secret (*phyi bar gsang*) refer to the place where the channels are located inside the body: on the surface, in the middle and deep inside.

[36] The channels that move up the fingers are connected with the essential organs. The channels that move down the fingers are connected with the hollow organs.

།དེ་ལས་གྱེས་པའི་པགས་པའི་རྩ་རྩ་འབྱམ་དང་སུམ་སྟོང་། །ཀུ་ཡི་རྒྱུན་རྩ་འབྱམ་དང་སུམ་སྟོང་། ། རུས་པའི་འཛར་རྩ་འབྱམ་དང་སུམ་སྟོང་། །ཁྲག་གི་འཕྱོ་རྩ་འབྱམ་དང་སུམ་སྟོང་། །སྲོད་ཀྱི་བཅུད་རྩ་འབྱམ་དང་སུམ་སྟོང་། །དབང་པོ་ཡན་ལག་གི་འཛིན་རྩ་འབྱམ་དང་སུམ་སྟོང་། །དེ་ལྟར་ཉི་ཁྲི་བརྒྱད་འབྱམ་མོ།

From these seven hundred and twenty thousand channels branch out:

- One hundred and twenty thousand[37] subtle channels in the skin;
- One hundred and twenty thousand continuing channels in the flesh;
- One hundred and twenty thousand channels that touch the bones;
- One hundred and twenty thousand channels in which flows blood;
- One hundred and twenty thousand channels in which flow the essences of the hollow organs; and
- One hundred and twenty thousand branch channels that guide the senses.

---

[37] Though the text says one hundred and three thousand, if we multiply this six times, it does not add up to seven hundred and twenty thousand. Therefore, instead we may have to read one hundred and twenty thousand.

།རྩ་ཆེན་ཚོན་ཐག་བརྐྱངས་པ་འདྲ། །རྩ་སྦོན་མཚོན་སྐུད་དྲང་པ་འདྲ། །རྩ་བཟན་དུ་བ་བྲེས་པ་འདྲ། །ཕྱི་རྩ་རས་གུར་ཕུབ་པ་འདྲ། །ནང་རྩ་ཐྲིན་བལ་སྦྲངས་པ་འདྲ། །ཤེས་རབ་དུན་པ་གསལ་བའི་མེ། །རྩ་ཡང་མང་ལ་གནས་ཀྱང་མང་། །སྦྲིན་པ་སྒུགས་པ་དབང་པོ་མེད། །རྩ་ཡང་ལྕུང་ལ་གནས་ཀྱང་ཆུང་། །རྩ་རེ་བཞིན་དུ་གནད་རེ་ཡི། །འཁམས་གསུམ་ཚམ་གྱི་སྐྱེ་གནས་དང་། །སྦྲིན་ཡོན་ཐབས་ཆད་ལུས་ལ་ཡོད། །སྲུང་ཕྲིད་འཁོར་འདས་སེམས་ཅན་གྱི། །སྐྱེ་ས་སྐྱེ་གནས་རྩ་ལ་ཡོད། །དེ་ཕྱིར་སྐྱོན་བཙས་ཡོན་ཏན་བསྐྱེད། །ལུས་གནད་སེམས་གནད་བསམ་ཡས་ཡོད། །འཕུལ་འཁོར་ལུས་སྐྱོང་འཕུལ་ཕྱག་ཡོད། །མཆོར་རྩ་ཁྲག་གིས་གང་ན་འཆི། །འོད་ཀྱི་རྩ་ལྟ་འགགས་ན་སྨྲེ། །དྲགས་མའི་རྩ་ལྟ་ཞར་ན་རྔུགས། །སྲུང་རྩ་མཐིས་པའི་གང་ན་བརྒྱལ། །ལྷག་རྩ་ཁྲག་གིས་གང་ན་གཞིད། །སྲོག་རྩ་རྔུང་ནི་ཞགས་ན་སྨྱོ། །ཡེ་ཤེས་རྩ་འགགས་དོན་དམ་འགྲོག །ཅེས་བྱ་སྟེ།

The major channels are like stretched tent ropes, the ministerial channels are like straight coloured threads, the minor channels are like a spread out net, the exterior channels are like a cotton tent that has been set up, and the interior channels are like cotton. Someone who is intelligent and has a clear memory has more channels and they function well. Someone who is stupid or dumb and has malfunctioning senses, has fewer channels that don't function well. Each channel has its specific function. All types of conception in the three realms of existence, and all defects and qualities, are present in the body. All places of birth of beings in the universe in samsara and nirvana are present in the channels. Therefore, correct faults and develop qualities (of the channels). There is an inconceivable number of key points for the body and mind. There are hundreds of thousands of magical movements for physical exercise.

When the channel of the spleen is filled with blood one will die. When the five channels of light are blocked one will be stupid. When the channels for pure essence are impaired one will be dumb. When the channels for wind are filled with bile one will fall unconscious. When the channels at the back of the neck[38] are filled with blood one will be sleepy. When the life channel is blocked one will go crazy. When the wisdom channels are blocked (realisation of) the absolute will be blocked.'

---

[38] (*sbag rtsa*) according to one explanation 'mixed channels', i.e. channels where a mix of blood and wind flow. According to another explanation *sbag rtsa* are the channels at the back of the head.

ཁམས་གསུམ་སེམས་ཅན་ཕྱིང་ཚོད་ཀྱི་སྐྱེ་བའི་རོ་བོ་དང་རྟེན་གྱི་རྩ་རང་ལུས་ལ་
ཡོད་པས། ཆ་གང་ཆེ་བ་རྩ་མང་བས་དེ་དེ་ཆེ་ལ་ལས་དང་ཉོན་མོངས་པ་ཡང་སྐྱེ་
བ་ཡིན་ཞིང་། དེའི་སྲུང་བ་དང་སྐྱེ་ལས་དང་རྟོག་པ་རྒྱུ་མཚན་ཆེའོ། །དེའི་གཉེན་
པོ་གསང་སྔགས་ཀྱི་བསྐྱེད་སྐོམ་ལུས་གནད་གོ་ཕྱུག་ཏུ་ར་ ཞེས་བྱུང་།

The body is the basic support and essence of birth of any type of sentient being in the three realms. The part (of the body) that is bigger has more channels. The bigger it is (i.e. the more channels there are) the more (related) karma and disturbing emotions will develop. This is the main reason for (experiencing) appearances, dreams and thoughts. For their antidotes study the meditation of the generation (and completion) stage and the key points for the body of secret mantra[39].

---

[39] This refers to the practice as explained in the second part of the manual.

གསུམ་པ་མི་ཟུབ་ཐིག་ལེའི་འཁྲུལ་པ་སྐར་རྐྱང་གི་སྲི་དོན་བཤད་པ་ལ། འཁྲུལ་བ་
སྐར། ཀུན་རྟོག་རྐྱང་དུ་གསལ་བ་ལ་གསུམ་སྟེ། རྐྱང་གི་རྣམ་བཞག་དང་། རྣམ་
གྲངས་དང་། རྣམ་དབྱེའོ།

།དང་པོ་རྐྱང་གི་རྣམ་པར་བཞག་པ་ཚམ་གྱི་དབང་དུ་བྱས་ན། ལས་ཀུན་བྱེད་པ་
ཡིན་ཏེ། ཀུན་ནས་ཉོན་མོངས་པ་འབྱོར་པའི་རྐྱང་དང་། རྣམ་པར་བྱང་བ་སྒྲུབ་ཉན་
ལས་འདས་པའི་རྐྱང་ཞེས་བྱ་བ། ལས་གང་ཞིག་སྒྲུབ་སྒྲུལ་དང་བདེ་བ་ཐམས་
ཅད་སྐྱེད་དུ་འགྱུར་བོ།

།རྣམ་གྲངས་ལ་ཡང་རྒྱས་བསྡུས་གསུམ་སྟེ། རྒྱས་པ་ཕྱེད་པའི་རྐྱང་རིན་པོ་ཆེ་ལས་
སོགས་པ་གསུང་རབ་ལས་བར་ལས་གསུངས་པ་ཉི་ཤུ་རྩ་ལྔ་པ་དང་།

Explanation of the winds

Third is the brief explanation of the winds in accordance with the commentary on the 'tigle that does not degenerate'. According to that commentary there are three topics to clarify (with respect to) relative wind *(kun dzob rlung)*: its exposition, enumeration and categories.

The exposition

First, merely from the point of the view of its exposition, wind is what makes everything function: karmic wind (makes) thoroughly disturbed emotions (function) and nirvanic wind (makes) complete enlightenment (function). Wind creates any type of the suffering and all happiness.

Enumerations

There are elaborate, medium length and condensed enumerations. According to the elaborate enumeration in the Buddha's scriptures such as the Precious Wind of Existence[40] there are twenty-five winds[41].

---

[40] The Precious Wind of Existence is a text in the Hundred Thousand Verses *(khams chen stong phrag rgya ba)*, i.e. the perfection of wisdom *(prajna paramita)* literature.

[41] This is the elaborate enumeration.

འབྱུང་དུ་གསང་སྔགས་མ་རྒྱུད་འདི་ཡི་དགོངས་པ་ལ་དགུ་སྟེ། བོན་ཉིད་ཀྱི་དབྱིངས་རླུང་རང་བཞིན་ཆོ་བོ་ཉིད་ཀྱི་ལས་བྱེད་པ་དང་། ཡེ་ཤེས་ཀྱི་པའི་རླུང་ཡེ་ཤེས་སྐྱེད་པའི་ལས་བྱེད་པ་དང་། རིག་པའི་རང་རླུང་རང་འབྱུང་དེ་ཁོ་ན་ཉིད་ཀྱི་ལས་བྱེད་པ་དང་། ཡིད་ཀྱི་རྟ་རླུང་འགྱུ་བྱེད་སྣ་ཚོགས་ཀྱི་ལས་བྱེད་པ་དང་། ལས་ཀྱི་ཕུགས་རླུང་བར་དོའི་ལས་བྱེད་པ་དང་། ཉོན་མོངས་པའི་རྒྱབ་རླུང་དུག་ལྔའི་ལས་བྱེད་པ་དང་། འདུ་བའི་འཁུག་རླུང་གནས་འཁྱུག་འཕེལ་འགྲིབ་ཀྱི་ལས་བྱེད་པ་དང་། སྲིད་པའི་སྟོབས་རླུང་གིས་སྟོང་བཅུད་ཕྱི་ནང་གི་ལས་བྱེད་པ་དང་། བསྐལ་པའི་འཇིག་རླུང་གིས་ཕྱི་ནང་བཤིག་པའི་ལས་བྱེད་པ་དང་དགུགོ།

In the medium length enumeration which accords with the meaning of the Mother Tantra of secret mantra there are nine (types of) winds:

- The winds of the space of the nature of existence, (that) naturally function as (support to abide in) the essence of the nature of reality;
- The winds of the bliss of wisdom, (that) function (to support) the generation of wisdom;
- The winds of awareness itself, (that) function (to support) the self-arising of suchness;
- The winds of the horse of (of the energy that moves) mind, (that) function as (support of) the variety of movement (of thought);
- The winds of the power of karma, (that) function to support (the activation of karma) during the intermediate state;
- The rough winds of the disturbing emotions, (that) function (to support) the five poisons;
- The winds that disturb the humours ('du ba), (that) function to support their disorder, increase and decrease;
- The strong winds of existence, (that) function (to support the creation of) the outer universe and inner essence (beings); and
- The winds that destroy the eons, (that) function (to support) the destruction of the external (universe) and internal (beings).

།དེ་རྣམས་རེ་རེ་ལ་ཡང་ལྟ་སྟ་སྟེ། བོན་ཉིད་ལ་ལྟ་ལྟ། ཡེ་ཤེས་ལྟ། རིག་པ་ལ་ལྟུལ་ལ་རིག་པ། དོན་ལ་རིག་པ། ལས་ལ་རིག་པ། འཕྲུལ་པ་ལ་རིག་པ། མི་འཕྲུལ་པ་ལ་རིག་པའི་རྐྱང་ལྔ། ཡིད་ཀྱི་ཏ་རྐྱང་དབང་པོ་སྒོ་ལྔའི་བདག་རྐྱེན་གྱི་རྐྱང་ལྔ། ལས་ཀྱི་ཕྱགས་ལ་བཟང་ངན་བཏང་སྙོམས་པའི་ལྷག་གི་རྐྱང་ལྔ། བོན་མོངས་པ་དུག་ལྔའི་རྐྱང་ལྔ། འདུ་བ་འཕྱག་རྐྱང་ལ་རྐྱང་མཆིས་བདག་གར་གསུམ་ལྷན་འདུ་རྐྱེན་བྱེད་གཉིས་དང་ལྷའོ། སྲིད་པའི་སྣོབས་རྐྱང་ལ་དག་པའི་སྲིད་པ་མ་དག་པའི་སྲིད་པ། ཕྱི་སྣོད་ཀྱི་སྲིད་པ། ནང་བཅུད་ཀྱི་སྲིད་པ། བར་མ་དོའི་སྲིད་པ་དང་ལྷའོ། །བསྐལ་པ་ལ་ཕུགས་རྗེ་ཤུགས་ཀྱི་བསྐལ་པ། འཕོར་བུ་ཆུང་གི་བསྐལ་པ། ཚེའི་བསྐལ་པ། དུས་ཀྱི་བསྐལ་པ། ལས་ཀྱི་བསྐལ་པས་བཞག་པ་ལས་སོགས་འཇིག་བྱེད་ཀྱི་རྐྱང་ལྔ། དེ་ལྟར་དཔྱེ་ནས་ལྟ་ལྟ་དགུ་ལས་རྐྱུ་གི་རྣམ་གྲངས་བཞི་བཅུ་རྩ་ལྷའོ།

There are five (winds) within each of these (nine):

- Five winds (are connected with) the five dimensions of the nature of reality;
- Five winds (are connected) with the five wisdoms;
- Five winds of awareness (function to) know the object, know its meaning, know its function, know delusion, and know non-delusion;
- Five winds of the horse of the (moving energy of) mind (function as) the empowering condition for the senses;
- Five winds connected with the wind of the power of karma are the winds (that function to create) good, bad, neutral, happiness, and suffering;
- Five winds that (function to create) the five poisons of the disturbing emotions;
- Five winds that disturb (the balance of) the humours are wind (humour), bile, phlegm, the combination of (two aforementioned) three, and all three can be the causal condition (of illness);
- Five strong winds (function to support) existence: pure existence, impure existence, existence of the universe, existence of beings, and existence in the intermediate state; and
- Five winds (function to support) destruction: destruction due to the era of the power of the compassion[42], small cycles[43], (the shortening of) the duration of life, time[44], and karma.

When one enumerates them in this way there are forty-five winds.

---

[42] When through the compassion of the Buddha ignorance, the two obfuscations and the twelve links of interdependent originations of sentient beings are eliminated.

[43] Small cycles (*khor bu chung*) refer to natural disasters like earthquakes and floods.

[44] The era of (the end of) time is when the universe is destructed by fire, water and wind.

།བསྐྱབས་པའི་རྣམ་གྲངས་ལ་གསུམ་སྟེ། སྲིད་པའི་རླུང་དང་། ཤྲན་སྲེས་ཀྱི་རླུང་དང་།
བསྐྲལ་པའི་རླུང་ངོ་། །དེ་ཡང་སྲིད་པའི་རླུང་ནི། སྲོག་འཛིན་པ་སྟ་གུ་ཤེས་པ་ལས་
སོགས་པ་འབྱུང་ལས་བཟད་པ་རྣམས་ཡིན་ནོ། །ཤྲན་སྲེས་ནི་གོང་དུ་བཟད་པའི་
རླུང་དགུ་ལྟ་བཞི་བཅུ་ཙ་ལྔ་འོ།

According to the condensed exposition there are three: the winds of existence, the innate winds, and the winds of meditation.

The winds of existence are the life-supporting wind, the winds that purify the inside of the channels and other winds that are explained in the perfection of wisdom literature (*prajna paramita*).

The innate winds are the five times nine winds or forty-five winds explained above.

།བསྐོམ་པའི་རླུང་ལ་བཞི་སྟེ། རང་འགག་དང་། རྩིས་འགག་དང་། བཙན་ཐབས་
དང་། རིམ་འགག་གོ། རང་འགག་ལ་གསུམ་སྟེ། མཐར་ཕྱག་གི་སངས་རྒྱས། ཆ་
མཐུན་གྱི་སེམས་དཔའ། ལྟར་སྣང་ནི་བསམ་གཏན་གྱི་སྐུ་རིགས་དབུགས་རྒྱུ་སྤྲོག་
མེད་པ་རྣམས་སོ། །རྩིས་འགག་ནི་ཉིན་ཞག་གཅིག་ལ་བོན་ཉིད་ཀྱི་དབྱིངས་རླུང་
ཉིས་སྟོང་བཞི་བརྒྱ། རིག་པའི་རང་རླུང་ཉིས་སྟོང་བཞི་བརྒྱ། དེ་བཞིན་དུ་ལྷག་མ་
བདུན་པོ་རེ་རེ་ལ་ཉིས་སྟོང་བཞི་བརྒྱ་རེ་རྒྱུ་བས། ཉིན་ཞག་ཕྱུགས་གཅིག་ལ་ལྷན་
སྐྱེས་ཀྱི་རླུང་ཉེ་ཁྲི་ཆིག་སྟོང་དྲུག་བརྒྱ་རྒྱུ་བས། དེ་དག་གི་ཉེད་པས་བདེ་སྡུག་
བཟང་ངན་ལེགས་ཉེས་དགར་འགྱོད་གཉིད་སད་སྐྱེ་འཆི་དུ་མ་འབྱུང་བའི་གནས་
སུ་བརྩིས་ནས་འགོག་པ་སྟེ་ཉེས་བྱ་ཕ་བས་རྩོགས་པ་དཀའོ། །བཙན་ཐབས་ནི།
རླུང་བྱམ་པ་ཅན་ཞེས་བྱ་བ་སྟེང་འོག་གཉིས་ཀ་བསྒྲམས་པ་སྟེ། ནད་བསྐྱེད་པས་
བྱ་བ་དཀའོ། །རིས་ན་རིམ་འགོག་ཏུ་བརྗོད་པ་འདི་ལ་བཞི་སྟེ། སྲོག་འཛིན་པའི་
རླུང་རིན་པོ་ཆེ་ཞེས་བྱ་བ་སྲོག་རྩོལ་བཅུད་ལ་འདོར་བ་དང་། སྲུ་གུ་སེལ་བའི་
རླུང་རིན་པོ་ཆེ་ཞེས་བྱ་བ་རྩ་སྦུབས་རྣམས་པར་བསེང་བ་དང་། སྔན་དུ་ཆེ་བའི་
རླུང་རིན་པོ་ཞེས་བྱ་བ། གཏུམ་མོའི་ནད་རྣམས་བྱ་གར་འཕྲིན་པ་དང་། བདེ་བ་
སྐྱེད་པའི་རླུང་རིན་པོ་ཆེ་ཞེས་བྱ་བ་དབུ་མའི་རྩ་ཁ་ཕྱེ་བའོ། །དེ་དག་གིས་ནི་རླུང་
གི་རྣམ་གྲངས་རྒྱས་པ་བརྒྱུད་ཁྲི་བཞི་སྟོང་། འབྱིང་བཞི་བཅུ་རྩ་ལྔ། ཐ་མ་གསུམ་
དུ་བསྡུན་ནོ།

There are four types of cessation of winds through meditation: natural cessation, cessation through counting, cessation through forceful methods, and gradual cessation:

- There are three ways for the winds to cease naturally: winds cease (upon reaching) final Buddhahood, for Bodhisattvas that are similar (to Buddha's), and for the gods that have mental stability for whom breath does not come and go.
- As regards winds ceasing by counting: during one day and night both 'the winds of the space of the nature of existence' and 'the winds of awareness itself' naturally move two thousand and four hundred times, and so do the seven remaining winds. Thus, during one day and night winds naturally move twenty-one thousand and six hundred times and function to create happiness and unhappiness, good and bad, right and wrong, joy and depression, sleeping and waking, and birth and death. When we count the winds they cease but because they are subtle it is difficult exhaust them.
- Forceful ceasing is vase breathing in which one holds the upper and lower winds. As illness may be generated it is difficult to apply.
- The four winds that cease gradually are: 'The precious life-holding wind' (that) vanishes into the essence of vitality. 'The precious wind that purifies the channels' (that) revitalizes the inside of the channels. 'The precious wind that is greater than medicine' (that) expels all illnesses (caused by wrong practice of) inner fire, through the hollow opening. 'The precious bliss generating' wind that opens the door of the central channel.

This explains the elaborate enumeration in eighty-four thousand winds, the medium length enumeration in forty-five winds, and the condensed enumeration in three winds.

།གསུམ་པ་རྐྱེན་གྱི་རྣམ་དབྱེ་ལ་གསུམ་སྟེ། ཚ་བའི་རྐྱེན་དང་། ཡན་ལག་གི་རྐྱང་
དང་། ཞིང་ལམ་གྱི་རྐྱང་ངོ་། །ཚ་བའི་རྐྱེན་ལ་དེ་ཞིང་བཅུང་ཆུ་ཚ་ལྟ་སྟེ། རྐྱང་གི་
ཏོ་བོ་ལྟ། གནས་ས་ལྟ། གཟུགས་དབྱིབས་ལྟ། ཞེད་ལས་ལྟ། དགོ་ནས་གཞི་ལྟ། ཁ་
དོག་ལྟ། ཕན་ཡོན་ལྟ། མེད་སྐྱོན་ལྟ། ཐོམ་སྟོབས་ལྟ། འགྱུར་སྐྱོན་ལྟ། འཛིན་
ཐབས་ལྟ། ཟིན་དཀགས་ལྟ། བོག་སྐྱོན་ལྟ། བོག་ནོན་ལྟ། སྦྱར་སོ་ལྟ། འཐས་ཐུ་ལུངའོ།
།དེ་ལྟར་རྐྱང་གི་དེ་ཞིང་བཅུང་ཆུ་ཚ་ལྟ་ཡོད་པ་ལ།

ཚ་བའི་རྐྱང་ལྟ་ནི། སྒོག་འཛིན་པའི་རྐྱང་རེན་པོ་ཆེ། མེ་མཉམ་གྱི་རྐྱང་རེན་པོ་ཆེ།
གྱེན་རྒྱུའི་རྐྱང་རེན་པོ་ཆེ། ཁྱབ་ཤེད་ཀྱི་རྐྱང་རེན་པོ་ཆེ། ཐུར་སེལ་གྱི་རྐྱང་རེན་པོ་
ཆེ་དང་ལྔའོ།

།གཞིས་པ་གནས་ས་ལ་ནི། །ཁྱེ་རྒྱུ་བྱང་ནས་སྐུ་སྒོ་ལྡང་པར་འབྱིལ། །སྒོག་འཛིན་
སྒོག་ཚ་སྟེང་དང་སྐྲོ་བར་གནས། །མེ་མཉམ་ལྟེ་བ་པོ་བ་རྒྱ་མར་གནས། །ཁྱབ་ཤེད་
མགྱིན་པ་ལུས་ཀུན་ཁྱབ་པར་གནས། །ཐུར་སེལ་བོག་སྐྲོ་ཀྱུ་འཁས་གསང་བར་
གནས།

Categories

With regard to the third topic, categories, there are root winds, branch winds, and sub-branch winds. The root winds have eighty-five characteristics (including the root winds themselves): five essential (winds), five locations, five shapes, five functions, five main intentions, five colours, five benefits, five absences, five powers of meditation, five defects of changing (into disturbing emotions), five ways to hold them, five signs of progress, five defects of going wrong, five ways to rectify, five connections, and five results. Thus the winds have eighty-five characteristics.

The five root winds:

- Precious life-supporting wind,
- Precious fire-equalising wind,
- Precious upward-moving wind,
- Precious pervasive wind, and
- Precious downward-clearing wind.

Second, the five locations:

- The upward-moving wind circulates from (within) the chest through the brain up to the nostrils,
- The life-supporting wind abides in the channel of life, heart and lungs,
- The fire-equalising wind abides in the navel, stomach and intestines,
- The pervasive wind abides in the throat[45] and pervades throughout the body, and
- The downward-clearing wind abides in the lower doors, at the bottom of the intestines and in the secret place.

---

[45] At the time of practice this wind is visualised in the central channel between the navel and junction, from where it radiates throughout the body.

།གསུམ་པ་གཟུགས་དབྱིབས་ལྟ་ནི། །ཁྱེན་རྒྱུ་གདགས་དང་འད་ང་སྟེ་ལྱ་བ་མས་
འདེགས་ཚེབས་གཉམ་གྱུས། །སྟོག་འརྗེན་རིན་ཆེན་འད་སྟེ་སྟོང་བུ་སྟེང་པོ་འོད་
ཟེར་བཅས། །མི་མཉམ་དབལ་ཁང་འད་སྟེ་དག་ཤུལ་རྗེ་གཉུམ་འབར། །ཁྱབ་བྱེད་
ཏེ་ཟེར་འད་སྟེ་ཕྱོགས་བཅུ་ཀུན་ཏུ་འཕྲོ། །ཁྱར་སེལ་སྐྱང་བ་འད་སྟེ་དབལ་ངར་
སྟོབས་ཤུགས་ཆེ།

བཞི་བ་བྱེད་ལས་ལྟ་ནི། །ཁྱེན་རྒྱུ་དཀུགས་རྒྱ་ཟས་སྐྱེད་སྟ་བར་བྱེད། །སྟོག་འརྗེན་
སྟོག་བཟང་རྦོ་སྟོབས་འདོད་པ་བསྐུལ། །མི་མཉམ་ཟས་འད་དོད་བསྐྱེད་ལུས་ཀུན་
གསོ། །ཁྱབ་བྱེད་ལུས་ཀུན་བྱ་བ་ཐལ་ཆེར་བྱེད། །ཁྱར་སེལ་གཉང་སྟེ་ཐིག་ལེ་
འབྱིན་སྟོམ་བྱེད།

Third, the five shapes:

- Upward-moving wind is like a parasol with the hub raised up from below and the spokes spreading out downward,
- Life-supporting wind is like a jewel of which the heart that is like a wick radiates light rays,
- Fire-equalising wind is like a stove with three fierce flames (inside it),
- Pervasive wind is like sun rays that radiate in all ten direction, and
- Downward-clearing wind is like a bellows that increases the strength of flames.

Fourth, the five functions:

- Upward-moving wind makes the breath move, and (allows one) to swallow food and speak,
- Life-supporting wind sustains life, (gives) power to the mind, and to realise one's wishes,
- Fire-equalising wind generates warmth to digest food, and thus nourishes the whole body,
- Pervasive wind functions to perform most physical activities, and
- Downward-clearing wind functions to expel or hold faeces and essential fluids (*tigle*)[46].

---

[46] In this case the gross aspect of *tigles*.

།ལྷ་བ་དགོངས་གཞི་ལྟ་ནི། །གྱེན་རྒྱུས་ཚངས་པའི་དབུགས་མཐོང་རྩོལ་བར་བྱེད། །ཕྱོག་འཛིན་ཆོ་རིང་དྲན་པ་གསལ་བར་འགྱུར། །མེ་མཉམ་བདེ་དྲོད་འབར་ཞིང་ནད་རྣམས་སེལ། །ཁྱབ་བྱེད་རྟུ་འཕུལ་ཕོགས་ཆགས་མེད་པར་སྟོན། །ཕྱར་སེལ་བདེ་བ་རྒྱས་ཤིང་ཚབ་བ་དབྱེ།

།དྲུག་པ་ལ་དགོ་ལྟ་ནི། །གྱེན་རྒྱུས་ཡི་རྕུང་ནི་ལ་དགོག་སེར། །ཕྱོག་འཛིན་ནས་མཁའི་རྕུང་སྟེ་དགར་བ་ཡིན། །མེ་མཉམ་མེ་ཡི་རྕུང་སྟེ་དབར་བ་ཡིན། །ཁྱབ་བྱེད་རྕུང་གི་རྕུང་སྟེ་ལྡང་བ་ཡིན། །ཕྱར་སེལ་ཆུ་ཡི་རྕུང་སྟེ་སྟོ་བ་ཡིན།

Fifth, the five main intentions[47]:

- Upward-moving wind makes the treasure of the pure dimension at the port of Brahma's overflow,
- Life-supporting wind gives long life and makes for clarity of mind,
- Fire-equalising wind makes the warmth of bliss blaze and dispels illness,
- Pervasive wind allows to manifest miracles without interruption or obstruction, and
- Downward -clearing wind increases bliss and opens the channel[48].

Sixth, the five colours:

- Upward-moving wind is the wind of earth and thus it is yellow,
- Life-supporting wind is the wind of space and thus it is white,
- Fire-equalising wind is the wind of fire and thus it is red,
- Pervasive wind is the wind of wind and thus it is green, and
- Downward-clearing wind is the wind of water and thus it is blue.

---

[47] The main intention (*dgongs gzhi*) refers to the main quality we intent to develop by practising and obtaining control over the winds.

[48] i.e. of the wisdom channel.

།བདུན་པ་ཐབ་ལོན་ཀླུ་ནི། །ཀྱིན་རྒྱུ་དབང་པོ་བསྐྱེད་ཅིང་མགོ་ནད་སེལ། །སྲོག་
འཛིན་སྲོག་ཚོལ་བསྐྱེད་ཅིང་ཤེས་རིག་གསལ། །མི་མཐུམ་ཟས་བརྙུལ་ལུས་ཀྱི་རུངས་
གུན་བསྐྱེད། །ཁྱབ་བྱེད་ལུག་ལག་སྟོག་འཕེལ་ལས་གུན་བྱེད། །ཐུར་སེལ་རོ་སྲུང་
གུན་འདེགས་སྟོབས་འཕྱག་འདོན། །

།བཅུད་པ་མེད་སྐྱོན་ཀླུ་ནི། །ཀྱིན་མེད་འཛིང་རིང་ལ་སྐྲགས་དབང་པོ་ཉམས། །སྲོག་
མེད་ཚེ་ཉམས་དུན་པ་མི་གསལ་འཆི་བར་བྱེད། །མི་མེད་ཟས་བཅུད་མི་བཟུ་འཐུ
སྐུག་སློག །ཁྱབ་མེད་ལྤང་བར་མི་ནུས་ཡན་ལག་བཀལ། །ཐུར་མེད་གཅིན་འགག་
རོལ་བཅས་ཏུག་འགག་འབྱུང་། །

Seventh, the five benefits:

- Upward-moving wind enhances the senses and dispels headache,
- Life-supporting wind enhances vitality and makes the intellect (*shes rig*) clear,
- Fire-equalising wind digests food and enhances the body's constituents[49],
- Pervasive wind increases the power of the limbs and (makes that one can) perform any activity, and
- Downward-clearing wind supports all of the lower body and dispels bloating and disorders of the stomach.

Eight, the five faults of absence[50]:

- Deficiency of the upward-moving wind results in difficulty in a stiff neck, dumbness and weak senses.
- Deficiency of the life-supporting wind results in the decrease of lifespan, an unclear mind and death,
- Deficiency of the fire-equalising wind results in inability to digest nutrition, diarrhoea, vomiting, and a bloated stomach,
- Deficiency of the pervasive wind results in inability to get up and disability of the limbs, and
- Deficiency of the downward-clearing wind causes blockage of the passage of urine, stones and constipation.

---

[49] Nutritional essence, blood, flesh, fat, bone, marrow, and *tigle*.

[50] Absence (*med-pa*) does not mean a total absence of the wind but rather weakness or deficiency of the wind.

དགུ་པ་སྐོམ་ཕོབས་ལྟ་ནི། །གྱེན་རྒྱུ་འཕར་དང་རྐེད་འཕྲི་ཞིང་ཕོན་དབྱངས་སྒྲོགས། །ཕྲིག་འཛིན་དགའ་སྟེ་དང་བསྒྱེད་ཡེ་ཤེས་འབར། །མི་མཐུམ་བདེ་དྲོད་སྤར་འདོན་ཆོང་ཞིད་སྐྱེ། །ཁྱབ་བྱེད་ཕོགས་མེད་གྱུབ་ཏགས་རྩ་ཆོགས་འཛིན། །ཕྱར་ཤེལ་འབར་འཛོག་བདེ་ཆེན་དང་ལ་སྒྱུར། །

བཅུ་བ་ནོན་མོངས་སུ་འགྱུར་སྐྱོན་ལྟ་ནི། །གྱེན་ལ་ཐུན་དང་ཕྲ་མ་བཀྲལ་ཆོག །རྒྱབ་འབྱུང་། །ཕྲོག་ལ་ནེ་སྲང་ཁྲོ་འཆོག་ཕོག་ལུས་འཐེལ། །མི་ལ་གཏེ་སྒུག་གཕིད་ཕོག་ལྡེ་ཕྲིང་གཏིབ། །ཁྱབ་ལ་ཐབ་དོག་གཆོད་འགགས་མ་ཕྲིན་ཞེན། །ཁྱུར་ལ་འདོད་ཆགས་མེ་འབར་མི་གཙང་སྒྱོང་།

Ninth, the five powers of meditation[51]:
- Upward-moving wind (gives the ability) to fly, makes you laugh and proclaim the melodious sound of the pure dimension of reality,
- Life-supporting wind generates joy and lets wisdom blaze,
- Fire-equalising wind makes the blissful warmth rise up and gives birth to emptiness,
- Pervasive wind makes various signs of practice come forth without obstruction, and
- Downward-clearing wind (gives the power to practise) blazing and dripping, and integrate in a state of great bliss.

Tenth, the five faults when (the winds) become the (cause of) disturbing emotions[52]:
- Upward-moving wind becomes lying, slander, idle speech and harsh words,
- Life-supporting wind becomes hatred, anger, and death[53],
- Fire-equalising wind becomes confusion, sleepiness, heaviness, and dullness,
- Pervasive wind becomes jealousy, harming (others), animosity, and theft, and
- Downward-clearing wind makes the fire of lust blaze and causes sexual misconduct.

---

[51] Meditation on the winds has the power to achieve below results.

[52] Until liberation we are under the influence of disturbing emotions. But here the emotions become excessive because the winds are disturbed.

[53] Literally it says separation of body and life.

།བཅུ་གཉིས་པ་ཞེན་ཧགས་ལྲ་ནི། །ཁྱེན་ཞེང་འཕར་དང་མཁབ་ལྲིང་ལྲ་གནས།
བསྒོད། །ཕྱོག་ཞེན་ཚ་རོང་སྒྲོངས་འཇུག་འདྲ་འཕྲོ་ཕྱེང་། །མེ་མཏུམ་མེ་དང་ཆུ་ལ་
འཇིགས་པ་མེད། །ཁྱབ་ཕྱེད་ལྲ་ཆོགས་སྤྲལ་བསྒྱར་ལུས་སུ་སྒོང་། །ཕྱར་སེལ་ཆགས་
ལམ་རྩ་འཕུལ་ཞབས་དང་སྒྲུ།

།བཅུ་གཉིས་པ་འཇོན་ཐབས་ལྲ་ནི། །ཕྱེང་རྒྱས་ལྲ་དབང་བསྒུམ་ཞིང་ཚོངས་ཕྱུག
འཕང་། །ཕྱོག་འཇོན་ཕེས་པ་སྒོང་ཆིང་བཞྲིམ་ཚུལ་ག། །མེ་མཏུམ་སྒྲིལ་གྱུང་རྒྱ་མཆ་
ཕྱག་ལ་གནར། །ཁྱབ་ཕྱེད་བཟུང་ཐབས་མགོ་ལུན་ཡན་ལག་བསྐྱམ། །ཕྱར་སེལ་འོག
སྒོ་དྲེ་བཙུམ་ཕྱེད་ཚུལ་ག།

Eleventh, the five signs of control (over the winds) are:

- The sign of control over upward-moving wind is (the ability to) fly, soar in the sky and go to the realms of gods,
- The sign of control over life-supporting wind is long life, (the ability) to transfer into another body, and to radiate and absorb,
- The sign of control over fire-equalising wind is that one cannot be destroyed by fire and water,
- The sign of control over pervasive wind is (the ability) to manifest various (miracles) and display (different) bodies,
- The sign of control over downward-clearing wind is (that one can engage in) the path of desire and that one will have miraculous feet.

Twelfth, the five methods to hold (the winds):

- To hold the upward-moving wind, restrain the nose sense and eject (the wind) through the crown chakra,
- To hold the life-supporting wind, relax the mind and dissolve (the wind in the central channel),
- To hold the fire-equalising wind, bring in the ocean towards the rock (while sitting) in cross-legged position,
- To hold the pervasive wind, contract the head, body and limbs, and
- To hold the downward-clearing wind, open and close the lower door.

བཅུ་གསུམ་པ་ལོག་སྐྱོན་ལྟ་བི། །ཀྱེན་ལོག་ལྷད་འཕྲིལ་མགོ་འཕྲོར་ཕོན་ཕོང་རྐྱགས། །ཕྲིག་ལོག་སྟེང་རྐྱང་ལོག་སྐྱོ་བརྗེད་བཀྱལ་ནད་འགྱུར། །མེ་ལོག་མཐིས་པ་སྐྲ་ཡ་དྲུ་ཆུ་སྐྲག །ཁྱུ་ལོག་ལྷུ་འདུས་ན་འཁྱམ་གྲམ་ཐུ་འགྱུར། །ཕུར་ལོག་དྲུ་སྟེང་སྐྱེན་ནད་མབལ་མ་ཤ།

།བཅུ་བཞི་པ་ལོག་ནོན་ལྟ་བི། །ཀྱེན་ནད་བཙོས་ཐབས་ཀྱེན་ཏུ་མེ་དྲང་ཕུར་མཐན་ཕོག་ཏུ་གཏད། །ཕོག་སྐྲང་བཀུ་མཐེ་ཏུ་ཞིང་ཆུར་སྲང་ཕུང་པོ་གཤུག ། །མེ་མཐམ་སྐྱམ་དུག་ན་སར་ཆང་སྒགས་བཀྱུ། །ཁྱུ་ཏྲེ་ཡན་ལག་བཀུ་ཅུག་བཀྱུག་བསྐུམ་ཇ། །ཕུར་སེལ་ལོག་སྐྱང་ཀྱེ་དྲང་རྒྱ་མཚོ་འཕང་ལ་གཏད།

Thirteenth, five defects[54] of going the wrong way:

- When upward-moving goes the wrong way the result is brain disease[55], dizziness, deafness, blindness, and dumbness,
- When life-supporting wind goes the wrong way the result is restlessness[56], madness, forgetfulness, and fainting,
- When fire-equalising wind goes the wrong way the result is bile disorder, jaundice, dropsy, and tumours[57],
- When pervasive wind goes the wrong way, the result is disease caused by a combination of the humours, being crippled in the legs or arms, contraction of the limbs and rheumatism, and
- When downward-clearing wind goes the wrong way the result is dropsy, tumours, and dysfunction of the kidneys.

Fourteenth, five ways to rectify winds that have gone the wrong way:

- To rectify (illness caused by) upward-moving wind, do not draw up but press downward and focus below,
- To rectify life-supporting wind, (take) massage, bath in water, and rest the body,
- To rectify fire-equalising wind, apply oil at the painful place and pat with cupped hands,
- To rectify pervasive wind, rub the limbs with oil, and extend and contract them, and
- To rectify downward-clearing wind, direct the lower wind upward and focus on bringing the ocean upward[58].

---

54 When the winds go the wrong way.

55 *klad 'khyil* is a disorder of the brain when wind is stuck and circulates in the brain.

56 Literally *snying rlung* means heart-wind, a wind illness in which there is too much wind in the heart. It makes one very restless and moody etc.

57 Tumour (*skran*) includes both non-cancerous and cancerous tumours.

58 i.e. draw the stomach towards the spine and upward.

།བཙོ་ཟླ་བ་སྟུར་སོ་ཟླ་ནི། །གྱེན་རྒྱུ་བདེ་ཆེན་དང་སྟུར་བོན་རྐྱ་ཡིན། །ཕྱོག་འརྗེན་
བོན་འཁོར་དང་སྟུར་རྟོགས་རྐྱ་ཡིན། །མེ་མཉམ་སྒྱལ་བ་དང་སྟུར་སྒྱལ་རྐྱ་ཡིན།
།ཁབ་བྱེད་ཀུན་དང་སྟུར་བ་དོ་བོ་ཉིད། །ཐུར་སེལ་གསང་བ་དང་སྟུར་བདེ་ཆེན་ནོ།

།བཙུ་དྲག་པ་འབྲས་བུ་ཟླ་ནི། །གྱེན་རྒྱུའི་འཁྲས་བུ་འཕོ་བས་ཆངས་བྲག་བཏོལ།
།ཕྱོག་འརྗེན་འཁྲས་བུ་སྒྱོག་རྩོལ་གནད་དུ་ཆུད། །ཁབ་བྱེད་འཁྲས་བུ་སྒྱུ་ལུས་སྒྱལ་
བསྒྱུར་ཤེས། །མེ་མཉམ་འཁྲས་བུ་རྩེ་ལས་འོད་གསལ་འཆེ། །ཐུར་སེལ་འཁྲས་བུ་
ཆགས་ལས་དངོས་གྲུབ་ཐོབ།

Fifteenth, the five correspondences:

- Upward-moving wind corresponds with the chakra of bliss; this is the body of reality, the *dharmakaya*;
- Life-supporting wind corresponds with the chakra of the empty nature of reality; this is the enjoyment body, the *sambogakaya*;
- Fire-equalising wind corresponds with the chakra of manifestation; this is the manifestation body, the *nirmanakaya*;
- Pervasive wind corresponds throughout the body; this is the essential nature (body), the *svabivakaya*;
- Downward-clearing wind corresponds with the secret chakra; (the body of) great bliss, the *mahasukhakaya*.

Sixteenth, are the five results (of mastery over the winds):

- The result of mastery over the upward-moving wind is (the ability to perform) consciousness-transference through the crown chakra,
- The result of life-supporting wind is mastery over vitality,
- The result of pervasive wind is that one will know how to manifest the illusory body,
- The result of fire-equalising wind is (the ability) to control dreams and clear light (sleep), and
- The result of downward-clearing wind is obtainment of the realisation of the path of desire.

དེ་དག་རླུང་གི་ལམ་གྱི་དངོས་གྲུབ་སྟེ། །ཡང་དག་འཐོབ་བྱ་རྩ་གནས་ལྷ་པོ་དེར། །རླུང་ལྔའི་ཐིག་ལེ་འདྲོངས་པའི་ཡོན་ཏན་ཀྱུན། །འོག་སྒོར་འདྲོངས་པས་བདེ་ཆེན་སྦྱལ་སྐུ་འཕོབ། །ཁྱི་བར་འདྲོངས་པའི་གསལ་བ་རྟོགས་སྐུ་འཕོབ། །སྲིང་ཁར་འདྲོངས་པས་མི་རྟོག་པོན་སྐུ་འཕོབ། །མགྱིན་པར་འདྲོངས་བས་བདུད་རྩོམས་མཚོན་བྱང་སྟེ། །བྱི་པོར་འདྲོངས་བས་བདེ་ཆེན་ཡེ་སངས་རྒྱས། །ཞེས་སྟོན་ཏེ། རླུང་གི་དེ་ཉིད་བཅུད་ཏུ་རྩ་ལྷ་གསལ་བར་བཤད་པའོ། །

These are the realizations of the winds while on the path[59]. The pure (or final) results are all the qualities (that one obtains) when one brings the *tigles* of the five winds to the five chakras. When you bring them to the lower door you obtain the great bliss of the manifestation body. When you bring them (from the lower door) to the navel you obtain the clarity of the enjoyment body. When you bring them (from the navel) to the heart you obtain the non-conceptual state of the body of the nature of reality. When you bring them (from the heart) to the throat you obtain the equanimity of actual enlightenment. When you bring them (from the throat) to the crown you obtain the great bliss of primordial Buddhahood. Thus the eighty-five aspects of wind have been clarified.

---

[59] These are temporary realisations that are obtained while on the path.

།གཉིས་པ་ཡམ་ལག་གི་རླུང་ལྟ་ནི། །གོང་དུ་བསྟན་པ་ཚ་བའི་རླུང་ལྟ་ནི། ཚ་གསུམ་
འབོར་ལོ་བཞི་ལ་གནས་པ་ཡིན་པས་ཚ་བའི་རླུང་ངོ་། །དེ་ལས་གྱིས་པའི་ཚ་ཆེན་
བཅུ་ཚ་བཅུད། མཚོན་ཚ་སུམ་བཅུ་དྲུག་ཏུ་ལ་གནས་པ་དེ་ཡན་ལག་གི་རླུང་ངོ་། །

།གསུམ་པ་ཉིང་ལག་གི་རླུང་ནི། མགོ་ལུས་ཡན་ལག་གི་ཚ་བདུན་བཅུ་ཉི་ཤུ་ འདུ་
བའི་ཚ་བཅུད་ཁྲི་བཞི་སྟོང་། ཚ་ཕྲན་བདུན་འབུམ་ཉི་ཁྲི་ལ་གནས་པ་དེ་ཉིང་ལག་
གི་རླུང་ངོ་། །ཐབ་ཡོན་ཚ་ཡེ་འགྲོལ་པ་ལས་རྒྱུ་པར་ཤུགས་ལ་གོ་ཕྱུག་ཏུ་ར། ཞེས་
བྱུང་།

Second are the five branch winds. Because the above-mentioned five root-winds abide in the three channels and four chakras they are (called) the root winds. From them the winds that abide in the hundred and eight major channels and in the three hundred and sixty visible channels branch out. These winds are the branch winds.

Third are the sub-branch winds. The sub-branch winds abide in the seven hundred twenty channels in the head and limbs, in the eighty-four thousand channels for the humours, and in the seven hundred twenty thousand minor channels. Study the commentary on the channels for a detailed exposition of their benefits and qualities.

གསུམ་པ་མི་འགྱུར་ཐིག་ལེའི་འཁྲུལ་པ་ལས། བཞི་བ་གསུང་དབང་ཐིག་ལེ་གྲུབ་པའི་ཆུལ་ལ་དྲུག་སྟེ། སྒྲུབ་པ་ལྨྱི་ཐིག་ལེ་ཀ་ག་བཞི་བཙུ་ཚ་ལྦ་དང་། སྲང་བ་ཕྱི་ཐིག་ལེ་བཞི་བཙུ་ཚ་ལྦ་དང་། རང་རིག་ནང་གི་ཐིག་ལེ་བཞི་བཙུ་ཚ་ལྦ་དང་། གསུང་དབང་གསང་བའི་ཐིག་ལེ་བཞི་བཙུ་ཚ་ལྦ་དང་། ཡེ་ཤེས་ལྟ་ཡི་ཐིག་ལེ་བཞི་བཙུ་ཚ་ལྦ་དང་། ཡང་དག་དོན་གྱི་ཐིག་ལེ་བཞི་བཙུ་ཚ་ལྦ་དང་། དེ་ལྟར་བསྡུས་ན་དྲུག་དྲེ་ན་ཐིག་ལེ་ཤེས་བརྒྱ་བདུན་ཅུའོ།

།དང་པོ་སྒྲུབ་པ་ལྨྱི་ཐིག་ལེ་གང་དུ་གནས་ན། གང་ལ་ཡེ་ཤེས་གནས་པ་ལ་ལུས་གནས། ལུས་གནས་པ་ལ་ཙ་གནས། ཙ་གནས་ས་པ་ལ་ཁྲག་གནས། ཁྲག་གནས་པ་ལ་ཞག་གནས། ཞག་གནས་པ་ལ་ཐིག་ལེ་གནས། ཐིག་ལེ་གནས་པ་ལ་ཟག་བཅས་ཀྱི་བདེ་བ་གནས། བདེ་བ་གནས་པ་ལ་མ་རྒྱུད་ཀྱི་མཁའ་འགྲོ་གནས། མཁའ་འགྲོ་གནས་པ་ལ་བདེ་ཆེན་ཀྱི་ཡེ་ཤེས་གནས་སོ། །ཁ་གནས་པའི་ཐིག་ལེ་བཞི་བཙུ་ཚ་ལྦ་སྟེ།

Explanation of the *tigles*

Third, with regard to the *tigles* the commentary on 'the indestructible[60] *tigle*' says: 'Fourth, there are six ways in which indestructible *tigles* come to exist:

- Forty-five *tigles* of the body, that has been created;
- Forty-five *tigles* of outer appearance;
- Forty-five *tigles* of inner self-awareness;
- Forty-five *tigles* of the secret swastika;
- Forty-five *tigles* of wisdom deities;
- Forty-five *tigles* of correct meaning.

In this way, when condensed there are six tigles, and when sub-divided there are two hundred seventy tigles.

First, how do the *tigle*s of the body, that has been created, abide? Wherever there is wisdom there is a body. Where there is a body there are channels. Where there are channels there is blood. Where there is blood there is fat. Where there is fat there are *tigles*. Where there are *tigles* there is ordinary bliss. Where there is bliss, there are the dakinis of Mother Tantra. Where there are dakinis, there is the wisdom of great bliss. Thus, there abide forty-five tigles:

---

60   Here *yung drung* has been translated as indestructible. It means unborn (*gyung*) and uninterrupted (*drung*).

ཕྱི་བོ་བདེ་ཆེན་གྱི་འཁོར་ལོ་བཞི་སྟེ། །གཡས་དཀར་ནི་ཕོ་ཤིག་ལེས་གསལ་བར་བསྐྱེད། །གཡོན་དམར་མང་རུམ་ཤིག་ལེས་བདེ་བ་བསྐྱེད། །ཅུང་རེ་སྐྱེད་པའི་ཤིག་ལེས་བཏང་སྙོམས་བསྐྱེད། །ཕྱུ་ཚམ་ཏི་ཀའི་ཤིག་ལེས་བྱང་ཆུབ་བསྐྱེད།

།མཐིན་པ་ལོངས་སྤྱོད་འཁོར་ལོར་བཀྱུད་གནས་ཏེ། །ཕྲོག་ཆོལ་སྒོལ་གི་ཤིག་ལེས་ཆེ་གཡང་འཛིན། །སལེ་སྒྲོན་མེའི་ཤིག་ལེའི་ཤུན་གསལ་ཏེ། །སྲུ་ཕྲུལ་སྲུ་ཆྱལ་ཤིག་ལེས་རུ་བ་གསང་། །ཁྱུ་བུན་ཆྱང་གི་ཤིག་ལེས་སྲུ་སྲུབས་གསལ། །བདུད་ཆེ་གྲོལ་བའི་ཤིག་ལེས་ལྷགས་དང་བཏོན། །ཁྲིན་ཆེན་ལྱུས་ཀྱི་ཤིག་ལེས་གཞི་མདངས་བསྐྱེད། །ཧྲོ་འཕྲུལ་ཕྱུག་གི་ཤིག་ལེས་འཕྲིན་ལས་བསྐུལ། །ཁར་པ་དཱུ་ཡེ་ཤིག་ལེས་ལས་སྒྲོ་འཕྲེད།

།ཕྲུགས་ཁ་བོན་ཉིད་འཁོར་ལོར་ལྷ་གནས་ཏེ། །ཉེ་ཕུན་ཕྲུགས་ཀྱི་ཤིག་ལེས་སེམས་ཉིད་བརྟེན། །ཁྲུ་ཆྱུག་དངས་པའི་ཤིག་ལེས་སྟོབ་བསྐྱེད། །རྒྱལ་པོ་དབང་གི་ཤིག་ལེས་སེམས་སྟོབས་བསྐྱེད། །ཡེ་ཤེས་དྲོད་ཀྱི་ཤིག་ལེས་ཡེ་ཤེས་བསྐྱེད། །ཁྱུང་བྱུང་བཅུན་པའི་ཤིག་ལེས་རྨོ་བཅུན་བྱེད།

Four *tigles* abide in the chakra of great bliss at the crown:

- The *tigle* of the white channel to the right generates clarity;
- The *tigle* of the red channel to the left generates bliss;
- The *tigle* of the *tsangri* channel of the brain generates equanimity; and
- The wisdom *tigle* of the crown generates enlightenment.

Eight *tigles* abide in the chakra of enjoyment at the throat:

- The *tigle* of vitality maintains life;
- The *tigle* of the clear lamp makes the eyes (vision) clear;
- The *tigle* of overcoming illusory sound makes (sound) clear to the ear;
- The *tigle* of misty wind makes (scent) clear to the nostrils;
- The *tigle* of liberating nectar increases (taste) on the tongue;
- The *tigle* of the great gift of the body generates radiant complexion;
- The *tigle* of miraculous hands achieves enlightened activities; and
- The *tigle* of freedom in the head opens the door to the path.

Five *tigles* abide in the chakra of the nature of reality in the heart:

- The *tigle* of the heart is the seat of the nature of mind;
- The *tigle* of the pure essence of the cuckoo[61] generates happiness;
- The *tigle* of the power of the king increases mental strength;
- The *tigle* of the warmth of wisdom generates wisdom; and
- The *tigle* of the stable swastika gives stability of mind.

---

[61] As the cuckoo is the herald of spring it symbolises happiness.

།སྤྲེ་བ་སྤྱལ་བའི་འཕོར་ལོར་ཉེར་གཅིག་གནས། །མཚོར་པ་ས་ཡི་ཐིག་ལེས་བརྟན་
པར་བྱེད། །སྐྲོ་བ་རླུང་གི་ཐིག་ལེས་ཡང་ཞིང་གཡོ། །མཆིན་པ་རྡོད་ཀྱི་ཐིག་ལེས་
མདངས་རྣམས་བསྐྱེད། །མཁལ་མ་ཆུ་ཡི་ཐིག་ལེས་བག་ལ་སྡུད། །མང་ས་ཤ་ཡི་ཐིག་
ལེས་ལུས་རྒྱས་བྱེད། །ཁྲི་སེག་དབུགས་ཀྱི་ཐིག་ལེས་རླུང་སྟོབས་བསྐྱེད། །ནེ་རམ་རྡོད་
ཀྱི་ཐིག་ལེས་ཐབས་ཅད་འཇུ། །ཏིང་ནམ་ཁྲག་གི་ཐིག་ལེས་གཞི་མདངས་རྒྱས།
།ཟག་མེད་ས་ཡི་ཐིག་ལེས་སྒྱགས་མདོག་གསལ། །རྒྱུན་མེད་ཆུ་ཡི་ཐིག་ལེས་ལུ་བ་
བཏན། །དངོས་མེད་རྡོད་ཀྱི་ཐིག་ལེས་ལུས་ལོང་སྐྱེན། །དཔག་མེད་ནས་མཁའི་
ཐིག་ལེས་བཏོད་པ་བྱེད། །གཞུངས་པ་འཇེན་པའི་ཐིག་ལེས་ཐམས་ཅད་སྲུང་།
།དཔགས་པ་གཞི་ཡི་ཐིག་ལེས་ལུས་རྩུངས་བསྐྱེད། །ཚིལ་བུ་བཅུད་ཀྱི་ཐིག་ལེས་མཉེན་
ཞིང་གཡོ། །གོང་ཆེན་ངུས་པའི་ཐིག་ལེས་ས་མཁྱང་བྱེད། །རྒྱུ་འགྱུལ་རྩ་ཡི་ཐིག་ལེས་
ལམ་དུ་བྱེད། །ཁྲེན་བུ་ཤ་ཡི་ཐིག་ལེས་གཉེན་སྐྲོ་བགགས། །ཀུན་བཅུད་ཁྲང་གི་ཐིག་
ལེས་ལུས་ཀྱི་མཁབས། །དངས་མ་བཅུད་ཀྱི་ཐིག་ལེས་ལུས་ཀུན་གསོ། །འབར་འཛག་
ཞུན་སྤྱད་ཐིག་ལེས་སྐྱེན་པར་བྱེད།

Twenty-one *tigles* abide in the chakra of manifestation at the navel:

- The earth *tigle* of the spleen makes (the body) stable;
- The wind *tigle* of the lungs (makes) light and mobile;
- The *tigle* of warmth of the liver generates a radiant complexion;
- The water *tigle* of the kidneys (provides) cohesion;
- The *tigle* of flesh makes the body develop;
- The *tigle* of breath increases the power of wind;
- The *tigle* of the heat of fire (gives power) to digest everything;
- The *tigle* of liquid blood increases radiant complexion;
- The unsubstantial *tigle* of earth makes the skin colour clear;
- The *tigle* of continuity of water stabilizes the regenerative fluids;
- The *tigle* of non-referential warmth ripens the interior (essential parts) of the body;
- The *tigle* of immeasurable space gives endurance;
- The *tigle* that follows the spinal cord[62] collects everything together;
- The *tigle* of the base of the skin generates the (seven physical) constituents;
- The *tigle* of the essence of fat gives flexibility and mobility;
- The *tigle* of the bones of the skeleton gives firmness and strength;
- The *tigle* that travels in the channel opens the channels;
- The *tigle* of the fleshy glands prevents risks[63];
- The *tigle* of marrow, the essence of all, (supports) the castle of the body;
- The *tigle* of pure essence nourishes the whole body; and
- The *tigle* of blazing and dripping, and melting and collecting, ripens.

---

62 More precisely it follows the backside of the spinal cord.

63 *gnyen sgo bkag* literally 'stops the door of danger', i.e. prevents the risk of an illness arising.

།གསང་བ་ཐབས་ཤེས་འཁོར་ལོ་བཅུད་གནས་པ། །ཐག་བཅས་བསམ་བསེའུ་ཐིག
ལེས་ས་བོན་འཛིན། །གལ་འཕྲུག་རྒྱུ་བོང་ཐིག་ལེས་ཏེ་ཆེན་འཛིན། །སྲིན་སྲུད་མཐིལ
པའི་ཐིག་ལེས་རཀྲ་བསྐོ། །རྒྱུ་སྲང་སྐང་བའི་ཐིག་ལེས་ཏེ་རྒྱུ་བཅུང་། །རྒྱུས་ཕྲེད་ཕོ
བའི་ཐིག་ལེས་ཕུ་སྟོབས་འཕེལ། །རྫ་འཕྱལ་ཞབས་ཀྱི་ཐིག་ལེས་ཀྱང་ཤེད་བསྐྱེད
།མཛོས་པ་རྒྱན་གྱི་ཐིག་ལེས་བ་སྤྲུ་འཕེལ། །སྲིབགས་མ་ཏེ་ཐབའི་ཐིག་ལེས་ཕུལ་ལས
ཤེར།

།དེ་ལྟར་སྒྲུབ་པ་སྐུ་ཡི་ཐེག་ལེ་ཡང་། །བཞི་བཅུ་རྩ་ལྔ་ཐམས་པ་ཡོད་པ་ལ། །གནས་ས
ོ་བོ་མཆན་ཉིད་སྲི་མེད་དང་། །ཡོན་ཏན་བསྒྲུན་པ་ལྟ་ལྟ་ལྟའི་དོན་ཆོང་བ། །ལུས་ཀྱི
ཐིག་ལེ་དེ་ཉིད་རྣམ་གྲངས་ནི། །ཉིས་བརྒྱ་ཉི་ཤུ་རྩ་ལྔ་ལ་ཡི་ལྔགས། །ཀུན་སྒྲུབ་འདི
སྲེར་མཐིའེན་པ་རྒྱལ་སྲས་ཡིན།

Eight *tigles* abide in the chakra of method and wisdom at the secret place:

- The substantial *tigle* of the reproductive organs (ovary and seminal vessel), controls the seeds (regenerative fluids);
- The *tigle* of the large and small intestines that moves and upsets, controls faeces;
- The *tigle* of the gall bladder that ripens and holds together, warms up blood;
- The *tigle* of the passageway of the bladder, controls urine;
- The *tigle* of the stomach that causes expansion increases the power of the flesh;
- The tigle of the magical feet generates strength of the feet;
- The *tigle* of the ornament of beauty makes the hair grow;
- The *tigle* of the smell-eater of waste purifies the rectum.

Thus there are forty-five *tigles* in the body that has been created. Each of them has five aspects: location, essence, defining characteristics, general name and quality. According to the Mother Tantra the number of *tigles* in the body is two hundred twenty five. One who knows (how) all has been created is a child of the Buddhas.

།ལྟ་བ་སྐྱེ་མེད་ཐིག་ལེ་ཡི་གེ་བཀོད་པ་ལ། །འགྲེལ་ལས། །བཞི་བ་ཡེ་ཤེས་དབྱིངས་ལས། ཡི་གེ་སྒྱུལ་བ་ནི། ཡེ་ཤེས་ཡུལ་ཅན་གསལ་བའི་ཆ་དང་། དབྱིངས་ཡུལ་སྐྱོང་ཉིད་ཀྱི་ཆ་གཉིས་ཀྱི་ཁྱེན་རྣམས་ལས། དབྱིངས་ལས་མ་བྲི་ཡེ་ཤེས་མ་ལྱུང་པར། ཕྱགས་རྗེ་སྨྲལ་བའི་རང་བཞིན་ཡི་གེ་བྱུང་སྟེ། སྒྲ་དག་པ། ཚིག་གསལ་ལ་བ། དོན་ངེས་པའི་འཕྲུལ་ཆེན་དུ་མཚོན་པར་བསྟན་པ་ལ། རྩ་བ་ཡང་དག་པའི་ཡི་གེ་བཞི་བཅུ་བྱུང་། ཞེས་དང་། དེ་ཉིད་ལས། ཡི་གེ་འཁོར་ལོ་རྟོགས་པར་བྱེད་པ་ནི། བོན་ཉིད་དབྱིངས་ཀྱི་གསུང་རབ་ཐམས་ཅད་ཀྱི་རྟེན་དུ་གྱུར་བ། མ་བྲིས་དོན་དས་རང་བཞིན་དབྱིངས་ན་བཀྲ་བ། ཡི་གེ་འཁོར་ལོ་རྟོགས་པའི་དཀྱིལ་འཁོར་དུ་བཞུགས་ནས་ཡོད་དོ། །གདུལ་བྱའི་དོན་དུ་རྗེས་འབྲིང་བཀོད་པ་མང་དུ་ཡོད་ཀྱང་། འཇིག་རྟེན་གྱི་འཕྲུལ་ཡིག་སུམ་ཅུས་གསུང་རབ་ཐམས་ཅད་ཀྱི་རྟེན་བྱེད་པ་བཞིན་དུ། དབྱིངས་ནི་དཀྱིལ་འཁོར་ཐམས་ཅད་ཀྱི་རྟེན་བྱེད་པ་ཡོད་དོ། །ཞེས་སོགས། ཆུལ་འདི་རྣམས་ཀྱི་འགྲེལ་བཀོད་སྐུ་གསུམ་རང་ཤར་གྱི་གཏུམ་མོའི་ཁྲིད་ལས་གསལ་ལོ། །

Explanation of the letters

Fifth, the letters are explained in 'the unborn tigle'. The commentary says: 'As to the fourth topic, letters manifest from wisdom and the pure dimension (*dbyings*). Wisdom is the subjective aspect of clarity and the pure dimension is the objective aspect of emptiness[64]. Due to the blessing of these two, from the pure dimension, while wisdom is not put in writing, as the manifestation of (their) energy, all letters naturally arise. The forty pure root letters arise and manifest clearly as great magical appearances (that represent) pure sounds, clear words, and definitive meaning.' From the same commentary: 'The wheel of letters that gives perfection[65] is the base of all the teachings of the Buddha on the pure dimension of the nature of reality. Without being written they (the letters) shine naturally from the pure dimension of the absolute. They abide in the perfect mandala of the wheel of letters. Even though there are many explanations on how to guide beings, the thirty magical letters of our world form the base of all of Buddha's teachings. In the same way the pure dimension is the base of all mandalas.' For a clear explanation consult the chapter on inner fire from 'The Natural Arising of the Three Kayas'.

---

[64]   In actuality there is no such subject-object duality in the natural state. So here the subjective and objective aspect are just a matter of presentation.

[65]   'The wheel of perfection of letters' refers the final thirteenth *bhumi*. It is the stage where one has achieved full Buddhahood.

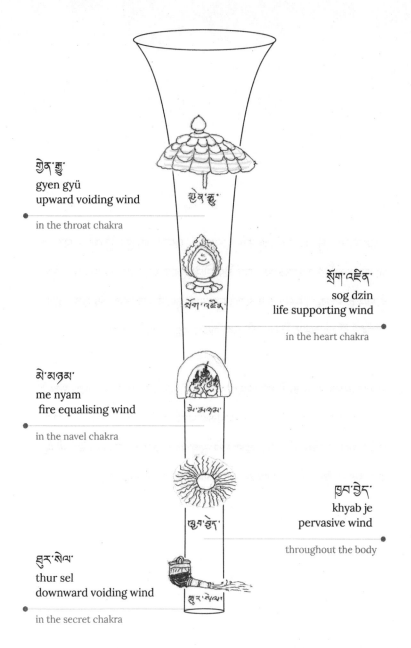

 གྱེན་རྒྱུ་
gyen gyü
upward voiding wind

in the throat chakra

གྱེན་རྒྱུ་

སྲོག་འཛིན་
sog dzin
life supporting wind

in the heart chakra

སྲོག་འཛིན་

མེ་མཉམ་
me nyam
 fire equalising wind

in the navel chakra

མེ་མཉམ་

ཁྱབ་བྱེད་
khyab je
pervasive wind

throughout the body

ཁྱབ་བྱེད་

ཐུར་སེལ་
thur sel
downward voiding wind

in the secret chakra

ཐུར་སེལ་

The original drawings of the five root winds by Yongdzing Rinpoche (2011), arranged into the central channel

གཉིས་པ་ལག་ཏུ་ལེན་པའི་ཚུལ་བཤད་པ་ལ། ཐབས་ལམ་ཁྱེར་ཀྱི་འགྲེལ་བ་ལས། འབྱུང་བ་ལྷ་ཡི་ལུས་བསྐྱེན་པ་དང་། ཐིག་ལེའི་དུས་གནད་བསྐྱེན་པ་དང་། ཨེ་ཤེས་རྒྱུ་བའི་ཚ་བསྐྱེན་པ་དང་། ནམ་མཁའ་དག་པའི་རླུང་གི་ཡན་ལག་བཞི་ལྷན་བསྐྱེན་པ་དང་། དྲོགས་སྟར་དམིགས་པའི་ཡུལ་གནད་བསྐྱེན་པ་དང་ལྔའོ།

།དེ་ཡང་འབྱུང་བ་ས་རྒྱུ་མེ་རླུང་འདུས་པ་ལས། རྒྱུ་རྟེན་འབྲེལ་འཚོགས་པ་ཆང་བའི་ལུས་འབྱུང་ཆེན་འབྱུང་ཆུང་དང་བཅས་པ་དངོས་སུ་གྲུབ་པ་ལས། ཤ་ཁྲག་དོད་དབུགས་བཞིས་ཡོངས་སུ་བསྐྱས་པའི་ལུས་འདི། ཚ་དང་རླུང་དང་ཐིག་ལེ་ཡི་གི་གནས་པ། སྟོང་གཞི་ནས་གསལ་བར་བཤད་པས་གོ་ཕྱག་བསྐྱེན་ནོ།

Part two

Explanation of how to practice

With regard to Part two, the explanation of how to practise, 'the commentary on the method: how to take the path of method' says: 'There are five topics:

- Explanation of the body (that consists) of five elements;
- Explanation of the key point of the time of *tigles*;
- Explanation of the channels where wisdom moves;
- Explanation of (the practice of) the four stages of breathing, pure as the sky;
- Explanation of the key point of the object of focus, as deep as the sky[1].

When earth, water, fire and wind gather and when all the causes of interdependent origination have come together, a complete body (consisting) of the great and small elements is actually created. In this body (that is) fully compounded of flesh, blood, warmth and breath, abide channels, winds, *tigles* and letters. You can understand this from 'the empty base', where it is clearly explained.

---

1   These five topics are related to the five words of 'the tigle of the elements'. This *tigle* is the root text for *tsa lung* practice. It reads *'byung ba'i thig le ye she nam mkha'i ngog'*, that may be translated as 'The tigle of the elements, wisdom (has) the depth (of the) sky'.

།དེ་ནས་འདིར་ནི་མངོར་བཤུས་པ། སྐྱེས་པའི་གང་ཟག་དེའི་བཅད་པ་ལུས་ཀྱི་གཞན་ཚམ་གཡིག་གིས་ཆོག་པ་ཡིན་ནོ། དེ་ལ་དང་པོ་སྟོན་དུ་འགྲོ་བ་མ་རྒྱུད་ཀྱི་དབང་དང་གདམས་ངག་དང་། སྐུ་མ་དགས་པའི་ལག་ལེན་དམར་ཁྲིད་ཞིག་ཏུ་བསྟེང་དེ། དཀའ་བ་ཉམས་སུ་ལེན་པ་ཡིན་པས། ཁྱག་རྟེན་གྱི་བྱ་བ་མ་ལུས་རྒྱབ་ཏུ་ཡིངས་ཀྱིས་འདོར། གསང་སྔགས་ཀྱི་དགེ་སྦྱོར་ཡིན་པས་ཉེན་ཏུ་དབེན་པའི་གནས་སུ་འཛུག ཉམས་ལེན་ལ་བར་ཆོད་མི་འབྱུང་བའི་བཟའ་བཏུང་གི་ཡོ་བྱད་ཚོགས་གས་སུ་བསགས། མལ་ས་རྒྱུང་ལ་བདེ་བར་འདུག་པ་ཡིན་ཞིང་། ལུས་གཉལ་བའི་བྱ་བ་བཀུ་མཉེ་སྦྱུག་པ་དང་། སེམས་འདུལ་བ་དང་དབུ་མར་འཇུད་པ་ཅི་ཤེས་ཀྱིས་སྟོང་པ་ཉིད་ཁ་འདགའ་བསྐོམ་པར་བྱ་བ་སྟེ། ཞེས་པས།

To summarize: it is sufficient for a meditator to just (have this) vital point of one body. For this first you have to make preparations: these are to receive initiation into Mother Tantra; to receive essential instructions; to receive the most essential instructions how to practice, in detail from a pure master; to abandon all worldly activities without exception because it is difficult to practise; to stay in a remote place of solitude because this is the positive behaviour of secret mantra; to collect food and drink so as to not interrupt your practice; to prepare a small comfortable bed; to tame the body by massage and rubbing[2]; to calm the mind and enter (the winds in) the central channel; and to meditate on emptiness for several days and nights as well as you know.'

_____

2   Rubbing with oil, e.g. sesame oil.

སྐབས་འདི་ཡི་བརྗོད་བྱ་རྩ་རླུང་ཐིག་ལེའི་རྣམ་བཞག་རྒྱུད་བཞིན་ཞིབ་ཏུ་ཤེས་པར་བྱེད། དེ་ཤེས་ནས་དེ་ལག་ཏུ་ལེན་པར་བྱེད་པའི་ཚུལ་ལ། གང་གི་ཆེད་དུ་རྩ་རླུང་ཐིག་ལེ་སྦྱང་བ་དང་། སྦྱང་བའི་ཚུལ་ཇི་ལྟར་བྱེད་པའོ། དང་པོ་ནི། བསྐྱེད་རིམ་དང་རྫོགས་རིམ་གཉིས་ཀྱི་ཉམས་ལེན་གྱི་ཆེད་དུ་སྦྱོང་རྒྱུ་ཡིན། བསྐྱེད་རིམ་གྱི་སྐབས་སུ་རྩ་རླུང་སྦྱང་བ་ནི། རང་གི་བསྐྱབ་བྱའི་གེགས་སེལ་དང་། བསྐྱབ་བྱ་པོ་གས་འདོན་པོགས་ཀྱི་ཆེད་དུ་དང་རྫོགས་རིམ་གྱི་ཆེད་དུ་རྩ་རླུང་སྦྱང་བའི་དགོས་པ་ནི། རྩ་གཡས་གཡོན་གཉིས་སུ་ཡོང་པའི་རླུང་རྣམས་རྩ་དབུ་མའི་ལ་ཕྱེ་ནས་དེའི་ནང་དུ་རླུང་བཅུག་པའི་ཐབས་བྱེད་པ་གཙོ་བོ་ཡིན། དེའི་ནང་དུ་རླུང་རགས་པ་འཇུག་མི་ནུས་པར་རགས་རླུང་རྣམས་དབུ་མའི་ནང་གི་ཕྲ་མོའི་རླུང་ལ་བསྒྱིར། དེ་ལ་བསྟིམ་པའི་ཕྲ་རླུང་སེམས་དང་འབྲེལ་བ་དེ་ཡར་སྟེང་ཁའི་ཐད་ཀྱི་དབུ་མའི་ནང་དུ་དྲངས། དེ་ཁར་དྲངས་པའི་ཕྲ་མོའི་རླུང་སེམས་དེ་བསྐྱེད་རིམ་གྱིས་བསྐྲབས་པའི་ལྷ་སྐུ་བསྟིམ་པའི་གཞི་དེའོ། །གཞན་ཡང་ཟག་བཅས་ཀྱི་ཐིག་ལེ་དབུ་མའི་རྩ་འཁོར་རྣམས་སུ་ཞུགས་གནས་ཐིམ་གསུམ་བྱས་པ་ལ་བརྟེན་ནས་བདེ་སྟོང་ཡེ་ཤེས་སྐྱེས་པ་དེ་སྟེང་ཁའི་དབུ་མའི་རྩ་འཁོར་ཀྱི་དབུས་སུ་གནས་པ་དེ་ལ་གོང་བཞིན་ལྷ་སྐུ་བསྐྱེད་པའམ། ལྷ་སྐུའི་རྟེན་དུ་གྱུར་པ་དེ་རིག་འཛིན་གོང་མའི་རྟེན་གཞིར་བཟུང་བ་སོགས་རྩ་རླུང་ཐིག་ལེ་སྦྱང་བ་ཕྱགས་ལས་དུ་ཉིན་ཏུ་གལ་ཆེའོ།

At this time (of practice) you have to know the exposition of the channels, winds and *tigles*, in detail in accordance with the tantra. Once you know this, in order to do the practice, (you have to understand) for what purpose and in what way to practise with channels, winds and *tigles*. First of all, there is a need to practise for the purpose of the generation stage or the completion stage. Practise with channels, winds and *tigles* during the generation stage (serves) the purpose to eliminate obstacles to realisation and development. The main purpose of the practice with channel, winds and *tigles* during the completion stage is to open the central channel and (get) the winds (to) enter it from the left and right channels. Because the gross winds cannot enter the central channel, they dissolve into the subtle wind in the central channel. After (the gross winds) have dissolved, the subtle wind that is connected with subtle mind is brought upward to the heart inside the straight central channel. The subtle wind-mind in the heart is the base into which the deity that has been practised during the generation stage is absorbed. Furthermore, based on the substantial *tigles*[3] entering, abiding and dissolving in the chakras in the central channel one generates the wisdom of bliss and emptiness. This wisdom abides in the central channel in the centre of the heart chakra and as said before the deity integrates into it or (put in another way) it becomes the basis for the deity. This is the residence of high knowledge-holders[4]. This is why the practice with channels and the reason is very important in secret mantra.

---

3 Here *tigles* refer to the potential of energy.
4 The four levels of knowledge holders are those who have realized complete maturation, power over life, the mudra, and spontaneous presence. The last two are high knowledge holders.

།གཉིས་པ་རྗེ་ལྟར་སྦྱང་བའི་ཚུལ་ལ། སྟོན་འགྲོ་དང་། དངོས་གཞི་ཨེ་རྗེས་དང་གསུམ། སྟོན་འགྲོ་ལ་སྤྱིར་དགོས་པའི་སྟོན་འགྲོ་དང་། སྐབས་བབས་ཀྱི་སྟོན་འགྲོ་དང་གཉིས། སྤྱིར་དགོས་པའི་སྟོན་འགྲོ་ནི། ཏིང་འཛིན་རྣམ་གསུམ་གྱི་དོན་ཚུལ་བཞིན་དུ་མཚན་ལྡན་གྱི་སྐྱོབ་དཔོན་ལས་མཉན། དེ་ཡི་དོན་གོ་བ་དེ་ལག་ཏུ་ལེན་པར་འདོད་པའི་དད་པ་ཅན་དང་། ལྷགས་ནང་མའི་དབང་བཞི་སྩོགས་པར་ཐོབ་པ་དང་། དེ་ཡི་དམ་ཚིག་དམ་པར་བསྲུང་བ་ཞིག་གོ།

གཉིས་པ་སྐབས་བབས་ཀྱི་སྟོན་འགྲོ་ནི། གནས་དབེན་པ་ཡིད་དང་མཐུན་པ། གྲོགས་བཀའ་རྟོ་བའི་བ། མགོ་མཐུན་གྱི་ཆས། གོས་རར་གཟན། ཨང་རག་སྟོས་ཐག གདན་འབོལ་བ། གཉན་དུར་དང་མཐུན་པའི་གོས། ཁམས་མཐུན་གྱི་ཟས་དང་། བཅུང་བ། ཁྲིད་ཀྱི་དཔེ་རྒྱུ། ལྷ་ཆ་མཆོད་ཆས་ཪྟེན་སོགས་དང་། སྐྱེན་ཆ་སོགས་ལེགས་པར་བསགས།

The second part of the text explains how to practise. It consists of three parts: the preliminaries, the main practice and the conclusion. The preliminaries consist of preliminaries that are required in general and preliminaries that are specific for this occasion. The general preliminaries are to listen to a qualified master who explains the meaning of the three contemplations correctly; to have devotion that wishes to practise what you have understood; to receive entirely the four initiations of mantra; and to maintain purely the sacred bond of samaya promises.

The preliminaries that are specific to this occasion are to find a remote place to your liking, a friend (retreat assistant) who easily understands your wishes, and to gather necessities like food, a cotton scarf, short pants[5], meditation belt, a cushion, clothes that are fitting to the season, food and drink that is agreeable with your constitution, guiding texts, requisites for the divinity, offerings, and medicine.

---

5   A skirt for the practice of magical movements (Tib. *ang rag*).

གཉིས་པ་དངོས་གཞི་ལ། ལུས་འདུལ་བའི་ཐབས་དང་། སེམས་འདུལ་བའི་ཐབས་
གཉིས་ལས། དང་པོ་ནི། འགྲོལ་ལས། དེ་ནས་རླུང་གནད་དུ་འཇུད་པ་ནི། ཚིག་ཕྱུར་
བསྡད། རོ་ད་སྐྱེ་ཤྱུར་བས་ཀྲང་པ་ར་རེའུ་མིག་བཞིན་དུ་བསྐྱེལ / ཕྱུས་མོ་བསྣང་བཞིན་
ཀྲང་པ་བསྐྱེལ། མཆན་། ། རྒྱང་གནད་དུ་ཅྱུད་པ་ཡིན་པས་སྐལ་ཚོགས་མདའ་སྐྱུག་
བཞིན་དུ་བསྲང་། བདེ་བ་བསྐྱེད་པའི་ཡན་ལག་ལྗེ་འོག་ཏུ་མཐམ་བཞག་ཕྱག་རྒྱས་
བཙོར། མི་རྟོག་པ་སྐྱེ་བའི་ཡན་ལག་མགྲིན་པ་ཐག་མདུད་བཞིན / ཆུང་ཚམ་བཀུག
མཆན། ། དུ་བསྲམ། ཤེས་པ་གསལ་བའི་ཡན་ལག་མིག་གཉིས་རྩ་རྩེ་ལ་གཏད། རྩ་
རྒྱང་གནད་དུ་བཟུང་བའི་ཡན་ལག་དཔུང་པ་ཁྱུང་གཤོག་བཞིན་ དུ་གདེངས།
རོ་ད་ཏིགས་ཤྱུར་བའི་ཡན་ལག་ལུས་སེམས་ཐམས་ཅད་རབ་ཏུ་བསྐྱིམས། ལུས་
གནད་མི་འཆུག་པའི་ཐབས་སྟོབས་ཐག་གིས་ལེགས་པར་བསྒྲམས། སྲང་བ་ཆེན་པོའི་
ཐབས་རང་ལུས་ཡེ་དག་དཀྱིལ་འཁོར་བསྒོམ་པའོ། ། དེ་ནི་ལུས་སེམས་འབྱུང་བ་
དབང་ལ་འདེབས་པའི་གནད་དོ།

The methods to control the body

With regard to the main practice, there is a method to control the body and a method to control the mind. Regarding the first the commentary[6] says:

- 'Stay in the rishi position to make the winds enter the right place;
- Cross the legs with the knees held up to generate warmth quickly;
- Hold the spine straight like an arrow in order for the winds to enter (the central channel);
- Firmly hold the hands below the navel in the equipoise mudra to generate bliss;
- Slightly bend the neck, like a knot in a rope, to generate a state without concepts;
- Focus the two eyes on the point of your nose to have clarity of mind;
- Extend the upper arms like the wings of a garuda to hold the channels and winds in the right place;
- Firmly hold body and mind to quickly have the signs of success;
- Bind the body with a meditation belt as the method not to loosen the key points for the body.

The great method for protection is to meditate on your body as the mandala of the meditation deity. These are the key points to bring the elements of body and mind under control.'

---

6   i.e. the commentary by Milu Samleg.

།ཞེས་གསུངས་པ་བཞིན་ལྱུས་གནད་དགུ་པོ་དེ་ཚུལ་བཞིན་དུ་ཞག་བདུན་གྱི་བར་ཉིན་རེར་ཐུན་བཞི་བྱེད་དེ། ཐུན་ལྔ་ཐུན་ཕྱི་ཐུན་སྦོད་ཐུན་དང་། ལུས་གནད་དེ་ལྟར་བཅས་པའི་དང་ནས་རང་ཉིད་མཁའ་འགྲོ་འདེགས་བྱེད་སྒྲོལ་མ་བསྒོམ་སྟེ། རྒྱུད་ལས། དང་པོའི་དུས་སུ་སྐྱལ་སྐྱེའི་ཏིང་ངེ་འཛིན། །འདེགས་བྱེད་སྒྲོལ་མ་ཐབས་ཀྱི་ལྷ་ཚོན། །སྐྲུ་རུ་བསྒོམས་པས་སྲུང་བའི་མཚོག་ཏུ་འགྱུར། །ཞེས་པས། མཁའ་འགྲོ་འདེགས་བྱེད་སྒྲོལ་མ་ལྔང་མོ་ཕྱག་གཡས་པས་གྲི་ཁྲག་དང་གཡོན་པས་ཐོད་ཁྲག་བསྣམས་མེད། དེད་བཞིའི་ཕྱི་ལུས་ཀྱི་དེད། ནང་ཚ་ཡི་དེད། གསང་བ་སྲུང་གི་དེད། མཆན་ དྱ་བགེགས་བསལ་བའི་བཟུ་ཡི་སྟེང་དུ་གར་སྦབས་ཀྱིས་བཞེངས་ཤིང་ཕྱག་གཡོན་པའི་གྲུ་མོའི་ཁུག་ཏུ་ཐབས་ཀྱི་བརྡ་རུ་ཁ་ཊྭཾ་ཁ་འཁྱུད་པ་པད་མ་དང་ཉི་མ་ཟླ་བའི་གདན་ལ་བཞེངས་པ། རིན་པོ་ཆེ་དང་རུས་རྒྱན་སྣ་ཚོགས་ཀྱིས་བརྒྱན་ཞིང་དར་གྱི་དཔྱང་ཕུ་འཕྱར་བ་མེ་རིའི་དུ་གུར་དུ་བཞེངས་པ་བསྒོམ།

In this way for seven days practise four sessions each day at dawn, in the morning, in the afternoon and in the evening, while you hold the nine points for the body and meditate yourself as *Degdje Drolma*. The tantra says: 'If from the beginning you concentrate on the manifestation body, i.e. meditate on your own body as *Degdje Drolma* who holds a trident (as the symbol) of method, this is the best protection'. The dakini *Degdje Drolma* is green-coloured, she holds a curved knife in her right hand and a skull-cup filled with blood in her left hand. She is in dancing position on top of four demons as the symbol of overcoming hostile interruptions. In the curve of her left arm she embraces a trident as the symbol of method. She stands on a lotus, sun and moon in the middle of a mountain-like tent of fire. She is adorned with jewels, bone ornaments and a silken scarf that is floating about.

དེ་ནས་རྩ་བསྐྱེད་པ་ནི། འགྲེལ་ལས། ཡེ་ཤེས་རྒྱ་བའི་རྩ་རྣམས་གསལ་གདབ་པར་
བསྟན་པ་ནི། རྩ་བ་གཅིག་དབུས་མཐིང་ནེ་ལོ་བསམ་གཏན་གྱི་རྩ་ཚངས་པའི་བུ་ག
ནས་གསང་བར་ཕྱག་པ། གཉིས་པོ་རྗེ་འོག་ཏུ་ཐུག་པ་ལ། གཡས་དཀར་དང་བསྐྱེད་
ཐབས་ཀྱི་རྩ་དང་། གཡོན་དམར་ཤེས་རབ་མང་ཆུམ་རྩ་གཉིས་འཁོར་ལོར་འབྱུང་
ནས་སྐྱེད་པའི་སྟེང་ནས་འཁྱིག་སྟེ་སྙིན་མཚམས་ནས་བརྒྱུག་ནས་སྙིམ་རེ་གཉིས་ལ་
ཐུག་པའོ། །རྩ་དབུ་མ་མཐིང་ཀ་སྨྲ་ཤྭག་ཚམ་གཅིག་ལ། གཡས་དཀར་ཤེལ་དཀར་
ཕྲ་བ། གཡོན་དམར་བྱུ་རུ་ལྟ་བུ། ཕྱི་སྤུག་མའི་ཚད་ཙམ་དང་ལ་འབྲིབས་ལེགས་པ་ར་
ཕྲག་ནས་ཁངས་ཁྱང་གཉིས་སུ་སྟོ་དོང་པའོ།

Then you visualize the channels. The commentary says: 'As for the explanation on how to visualize the channels where wisdom moves: the single blue central channel of contemplation (runs) from the opening of the port of brahma down to the secret place where the two (side channels) enter it. The right channel of method, that is white, and the red channel of discriminating wisdom, that is red, embrace[7] (the central channel) at the chakra-wheels, bent at the (top of the) brain and (after meeting) the brows exit at the nostrils. The central channel is light blue and (the size of) a walking stick, the right channel is white like crystal, and the left channel is red like coral. Both (side channels) are straight like bamboo and well formed. They go through the hollow behind the ears and exit at the nostrils.

---

7 Literally embrace. The explanation is that the side channels touch the central channel at the place of the chakras.

།རྩ་འདབ་ཀྱང་ལྟ་དང་མཐུན་པར་སྐྱི་བོ་བདེ་ཆེན་འཁོར་ལོ་རྩ་འདབ་སུམ་ཅུ་སོ་གཉིས། མགྲིན་པ་ལོངས་སྤྱོད་འཁོར་ལོ་ལ་རྩ་འདབ་བཅུ་དྲུག ཐུགས་ཁ་ཆོས་ཉིད་ཀྱི་འཁོར་ལོ་ལ་རྩ་འདབ་བཅུ་གཉིས། ལྟེ་བ་སྤྲུལ་པའི་འཁོར་ལོ་ལ་རྩ་འདབ་དྲུག་ཅུ་རྩ་བཞི། ལྟེ་འོག་ཐབས་ཤེས་འཁོར་ལོ་ལ་རྩ་འདབ་བཞི། ཡེ་ཤེས་རྒྱ་བའི་རྩ་དེ་རྣམས་ལས་གཞན་བསྒྱིས་པའི་ཆད་མེད་པས། ཞེས་སོ།

The petals of the chakras correspond to the (number of) deities. At the crown is the chakra-wheel of great bliss with thirty-two petals. At the throat is the chakra-wheel of enjoyment with sixteen petals. At the heart is the chakra-wheel of suchness with twelve petals. At the navel is the chakra-wheel of emanation with sixty-four petals. Below the navel[8] is the chakra-wheel of method and wisdom with four petals[9]. There is no limit to (the number of) channels you can meditate as coming from the channels where wisdom moves.

---

8   The colours of the chakras from the crown chakra downwards are white, green, red, yellow and blue.

9   The number of petals of the chakras is related to the deities in the Magyu mandala. On the path of integration when visualising the body mandala the following deities are visualised on the petals:
  - Thirty-two Dakinis of Immeasurable Compassion on the thirty-two petals of the crown chakra.
  - Sixteen Goddesses of Uninterrupted Compassion on the sixteen petals of the throat chakra.
  - Four Secret Mothers of Great Bliss and the Eight Ladies of Uninterrupted Great Bliss on the twelve petals of the heart chakra.
  - Sixty Offering Dakinis (five times twelve) and Four Dakinis who Perform the Real Objective on the sixty-four petals of the navel chakra.
  - The four Mothers of the Path of Integration on the four petals of the chakra below the navel.

ཚ་འབོར་རྣམས་དབུ་མ་དང་སྒྱུབས་འབྲེལ་ཞིང་མེ་ཏོག་གི་འདབ་མ་ལྟར་རེག་ལ་
མ་འབྱར་བལོ། །ཚ་འབོར་ལ་ཡི་གེ་པའམ། ཚ་འབོར་རྣམས་ཀྱི་གྱེས་གཞིའི་དབུ་
མའི་ནང་དུ་མཁའ་འགྲིང་རིགས་ལྔ་རིམ་བཞིན་ཡས་ནས་མར་མཁའ་འགྲིང་
དཀར་པོ། སྔུ་རྐྱང་དཀར་པོ། སྔུ་ཡང་དེ་པོ། སྔུ་སངས་གྱུང་རྒྱལ། སྔུ་མེད་མཐའ་ཡས།
ལྟ་པོ་དེ་སྐུ་མདོག་ཕྱག་མཚན་གདན་ཕྲི་དང་བཅས་པ་བསྐྱེད་པའམ།

The chakras are connected to the empty inside of the central channel and the petals touch one another without sticking together, like the petals of a flower. In the centre of the chakras or inside the central channel where the chakras branch out are the five *Khagying* from top to bottom:

- White *Khagying Karpo* in the crown chakra.
- (White) *Mugyung Karpo* in the throat chakra;
- (Green) *Muyang Debo* in the hart chakra;
- (Red) *Musang Gunggyal* in the navel chakra; and
- (Blue) *Mume Thaye* in the secret chakra.

Visualise these five with their body colour, hand implements, and throne.

ཡང་ན་སྤྱི་བོ་ལྷ་མ་བོན་སྐུ་ཀུན་ཏུ་བཟང་པོ། མགྲིན་པར་རྫོགས་སྐུ་མཁའ་འགྱིང་། ཐུགས་ཁར་གསང་མཆོག་སྙེ་བར་སྤྱུལ་སྐུ་འཆི་མེད། ཐབས་ཤེས་རབ་ལ་བཟང་བཟའ་བསྐྱེད་པ་ཡིན་ནོ། །དེ་ལྟར་ལུས་གནད་དགུ་དང་རླ་འདེགས་བྱེད་སློན་མ་བསྒོམ། རྩ་བསྐྱེད་རྩ་འཁོར་རླ་དང་བཅས་པ་ཆུལ་བཞིན་དུ་ཉེན་རེར་ཐུན་བཞི་རེར་སྦྱང་ཞིང་། ཐུན་རེའི་ཡུན་ཚོད་ཆུ་ཚོད་ཕྱེད་ཚམ་རེ་ཉེན་དང་པོ་དང་། ཉེན་གཉིས་པ་ནས་སྐར་མ་བཅོ་ལྔ་ཚམ་རེ་སྤར་བཞིན་ཉེན་གསུམ་སྦྱང་པ་དང་། དེ་ཡི་རིང་རླ་ཐུན་དང་ཕྱི་ཐུན་གང་བདེའི་བར་དུ་བཀུ་མཉེ་བྱ་སྟེ། ཐོག་མར་ལུས་ཡན་ལག་དང་བཅས་པ་ཆུ་རྡོན་གྱིས་བཀུས་སྟེང་། བཀུ་མཉེའི་སྐྲན་རྫས་བཟོས་པའི་ཏིལ་མར་གྱིས་ལུས་ཡན་ལག་བཅས་པ་ལེགས་པར་འཕུར་བར་བྱེད།

Alternatively, you can visualise[10]:

- Dharmakaya Guru Kuntu Zangpo in the crown;
- Sambogakaya White Khagying in the throat;
- Sangchog Gyalpo in the heart;
- Nirmanakaya Chime Tsugpu in the navel; and
- Zangza Ringtsun at the chakra of method and wisdom below the navel.

In this way you meditate (while keeping) the nine key points for the body and (visualizing) the deity *Degdje Drolma*. Practice four times a day visualizing the channels and chakras. Start the first day with duration of about half an hour. Add fifteen minutes on the second day and again fifteen minutes on the third day. In between sessions, in the morning or in the afternoon, massage the body including the limbs. First wash the body with warm water. Then rub it well with sesame oil mixed with medicine.

---

10 The five *Khagying* are the peaceful aspects of the five main deities of Mother Tantra:
- In the crown chakra is Khagying Karpo (*mkha 'gying dkar po* - White One Soaring in the Sky) with one face and four arms, abiding in sambhogakaya form on a seat of crystal lions. The first right hand holds a swastika at the heart. The second right hand turns a wheel. The first left hand is in equipoise and holds the stem of a lotus and the last hand holds a precious jewel.
- In the throat chakra is white Mugyung karpo (*mu rgyung dkar po*) holding a swastika at his heart in his first right hand and a vase in his left hand that is in the equipoise. The second two hands hold an iron chain and a flower.
- In the hart chakra is green Muyang Debo (*mu ye de bo*) holding a wheel and vase in his first two hands and a standard and utpala flower in his next two hands.
- In the navel chakra is red Musang Gunggyal (*mu sangs gung rgyal*) holding a lotus and vase in his first two hands and a light and the stem of a lotus in his next two hands.
- In the secret chakra is blue Mume Thaye (*mu med mtha' yas*) holding a precious jewel and vase in the first two hands and a water moon and halo flower in his next two hands.

ཉིན་བཞི་པ་ནས་སྦྱར་བཞིན་ལུས་གནད་ལྟ་བསྒོམ་རྩ་བསྐྱེད་ཕྱུས་པའི་སྟེང་དུ། ། ཀླུང་ཡན་ལག་བཞི་ལྡན་བསྒོམ་སྟེ། ཀླུང་རྩུབ་པ་དང་། དགངས་པ་དང་། གཞིལ་བ་དང་། འཕང་པ་དང་བཞི།

དང་པོ་རྩུབ་དྲུག་བསལ་བ་ནི། ། དང་པོ་སྣ་བུག་གཡས་པ་སྟིན་ལག་གཡོན་པས་མནན་ནས་རྩུང་སྣ་བུག་གཡོན་ནས་ཧྲུབ་གཡས་ནས་འཐང་བ་ཐེངས་གསུམ། ཀླུང་དེས་ཞེ་སྡང་ལས་གྱུར་པའི་ནད་གདོན་སྒྲིབ་པ་ཐམས་ཅད་བུན་ཀྱིས་སོང་བར་བསམ། ཡང་སྣ་བུག་གཡོན་པ་སྟིན་ལག་གཡས་པས་མནན་ཏེ་གཡས་ནས་ཧྲུབ་གཡོན་ནས་བཏང་བ་ཐེངས་གསུམ། དེ་དུས་རྩུང་དེས་འདོད་ཆགས་ལས་གྱུར་པའི་སྒྲིབ་པ་ཐམས་ཅད་སངས་ཀྱིས་བྱུད་པར་བསམ། ཡང་སྣ་བུག་གཉིས་ཀ་ནས་ཧྲུབ་སྟེ་གཉིས་ཀ་ནས་འཐང་བ་ཐེངས་གསུམ། དེ་ཡི་ཚེ་རྩུང་དེས་གཏི་མུག་ལས་གྱུར་པའི་ནད་གདོན་སྒྲིབ་པ་ཐམས་ཅད་སངས་ཀྱིས་བྱུད་པར་བསམ།

དེ་ནས་སྣ་བུག་གཉིས་ནས་འཇམ་ལ་རིང་བའི་རྩུང་ལྔགས་ཀྱུ་བཞིན་དུ་བཀུག་པའོ། །དེ་ཡི་རྩུང་རང་གནས་ཀྱི་རྩ་ལ་ཚུད་པའོ། །དྲག་རྩུབ་དུ་བྱས་ན་གནན་དུ་ཕྱེར་པའོ། །དེ་ནི་རྩུང་ཧྲུབ་པ་སྟིན་བལ་ལྟ་བུའི་རྩུང་ངོ་། །དེ་ནས་བཟུང་བའི་དུས་སུ་ཚ་གཉིས་ནས་མར་ན་ར་ར་སོང་བས་དབུ་མར་ལྔད་ཀྱིས་གང་བར་བསམས་སོ། །དེ་ནི་དགངས་པ་བདུད་རྩི་ལྔ་བུའི་རྩུང་ངོ་། །དེ་ནས་གཞིལ་བ་ནི། རྩུང་ཐུབ་ཐུབ་ཏུ་དྲག་པར་མནན། མི་ཐུབ་པ་ལ་ཧྲུབ་ཆུང་དུ་བྱ་ཞིང་དབུ་མ་ལ་བསྟིམ་མོ། །དེ་ནི་གཞིལ་བའི་རྩུང་མེ་དཔུང་ལྟ་བུའོ། །དེ་ནས་མི་ཐུབ་པའི་དུས་སུ་དངོས་སུ་སྣ་བུག་གཉིས་ནས་དལ་བུས་བཏང་ཞིང་། །དམིགས་པས་དབུ་མའི་ནང་ནས་སྟོ་ཕུ་ར་ར་འགྲོ་བར་བསམ་ཞིང་ལྔག་མ་ཆད་ན་ཡང་བསལ་པོ། །དེ་ནི་འཕང་པ་དུ་བ་ལྔ་བུའི་རྩུང་ངོ་། །

From the fourth day onwards, as before hold the key points for the body, visualize the divinity, generate the chakras, and on this basis meditate with the four aspects of breathing: inhale, open hold, pressing down and exhale.

First, purify foul air: press the right nostril with the left ring finger and three times inhale through the left nostril and exhale through the right nostril. Consider that with this (exhalation of) wind all illnesses, spirits and obscurations caused by anger vanish. Then press the left nostril with the right ring finger and inhale three times through the right nostril and exhale through the left nostril. Consider that with this (exhalation of) wind all (illnesses, spirits and) obscurations caused by attachment vanish. Then inhale three times through both nostrils and exhale three times through both nostrils. Consider that with this (exhalation of) wind all illnesses, spirits and obscurations caused by confusion vanish.

Then gather the wind through both nostrils, softly and slowly, bent like an iron hook. In this way the wind enters at the right place in the (central) channel. If you do this in a strong and rough way the wind will be go in the wrong way. This is inhalation, like silk. Then, when holding: consider that the wind that has gone downward evenly through the two (side) channels, enters and completely fills the central channel. This is open holding of the wind, like nectar. Then pressing: strongly press the wind as long as you can. When you cannot (press) any longer inhale a little bit and dissolve the breath in the central channel. This is pressing the wind, like a heap of fire. Then, when you cannot (hold and press) any longer, exhale softly through both nostrils. You consider that (wind) goes through the central channel like bluish smoke and you hold a little bit (at the end). This is exhaling like smoke.

ཀ་བདུན་གྱི་བར་དུ་ཐུན་རེར་རྐྱང་ཁྱགས་བདུན་ལ་རྐྱང་ཐུན་རེ་བཙིས་ཁ
ཐུན་གསུམ་རེ་ཚམ་དང་། ཐུན་གྱི་འགྱོར་དགོངས་སྐྱོད་རྣམ་གསུམ་དང་
རྒྱབས་མེམས་རྣམས་ཆུལ་བཞིན་བྱེད། དུག་རྐྱང་དགུ་པོ་ཡང་ཟྭ། རྐྱང་དུ་ཚང་གི
དུག་ཕུལ་མ་ཡིན་པར་སྐྱོམས་པར་བྱེད་བཞིན་སྤྱུང་ངོ་།

གཉིས་པ་འདྲེན་པ་སྐྱུ་ཡི་གནད་ཀྱིས་རྩ་ལམ་སྦྱང་པ་ནི། སྤར་བཞིན་ལུས་ཀྱི་སྡུངས་
ར་ལྟ་དང་རྩ་རྐྱང་རྣམས་ཚར་རེ་སྦྱང་བཞིན་པའི་སྟེང་དུ། ཀྱྭ་མ་དགྱེས་པའི་འགྱིང་
རེང་ཞེས་པ་དེ་དེང་གིས་སྟོངས་བཀྱེད། ཡི་དགམ་འཛུམ་པའི་བསྒུམས་འབོད་ཅེས་པ།
དུ་ཧུ་གིས་གནན་ལ་དབབ། མགས་འགྲོ་འབོད་པའི་བར་སྐུང་ཆེས་པ། ཧུ་དྲི་ཡིས་
སྤར་འདོན་བྱེད། ཡང་ན་ཨ་ཡོ་ཞེས་པས་དབངས་དམར་བ་ཡར་ལ་འདེགས་པ་
དང་། ཨ྄ོ་ཧུ་ཞེས་པས་ཆད་ཅིང་འགྲོ་མཐུད་པ་དང་། འདི་རྣམས་ཆགས་ལེན་གྱི
གནད་ལ་པོགས་འདོན་པའི་ཆེད་དང་། མགོ་ན་བ་ལ་འབིག་བྱེད་འབྲུ་གཅིག་དྲག
གིས་དྲངས་པ་དང་། འགྲོ་བ་ལ་ཧཱི་ཞེས་པས་མར་བརྟེག་སྦྲོ་སྦྲེང་རོ་སྐྱོང་ན་བ་ལ་དུ
ཕུས། ཞེས་འབུད། རྒྱབ་ན་གཟེར་བ་ལ། དུ་མང་། བང་ན་ཞིང་གཟེར་བ་ལ། ཕུ་མང་།
འཐམ་པ་ལ་པཏུཀྱིས་དགམ། འཕོར་ན། ཧཱི་གིས་སྤུང། སྲབ་ན་ཧས་ཀྱིས་འཐུག དེ
ལས་སོགས་པའི་སྐྱ་སྐད་སྣ་ཚོགས་པས་མི་བདེ་བ་ཀུན་དྲང་བར་བྱུ། དེས་རྩ
གནས་འཁགས་པ་དང་འཁྱིམས་པ་དང་། རེང་བའི་ནད་དང་གེགས་ཀུན་བྱང་བར
འགྱུར་རོ།

Seven breaths are considered to constitute one session of breathing practice and you practise three sessions of breathing practice each meditation session for the duration of seven days. At the start of each meditation session practise the Three States of Mother Tantra, refuge and bodhicitta. You also do the nine purification breathings. Practise evenly and not too strong.

Second, training the pathways of the channels by way of guiding sounds. As before, hold the position of the body, clearly visualise (yourself as) the meditation deity, and visualise the channels and the winds. On this basis, generate strength with HI HING, the long majestic sound for pleasing the spiritual master. With HU HUNG, the short sound smiling to the meditation deity, you bring (things) together and everything falls into place. With HUNG HRI, the symbolic sound for calling the dakini, you raise (things up). Alternatively, you make rise up what is low with A YANG, and with OM HUM you can connect what has been disconnected. These sounds (above) are meant to develop the key point of practice.

In case of headache, dispel it with HIK. In case of a floating state of mind, ground it with HAM. In case the lungs, heart or upper part of the body hurt, say HA HU. In case the back hurts (cure it with) HA MANG. In case the chest hurts (cure it with) PHOE MANG. When (feeling) dull, wake up with PHAT. When your mind is dispersed, collect it with HUNG. Thus, with various sounds you can cure all kinds of discomfort. With these (practices) you purify blockages and slackness of the channels, as well as long-term diseases and disturbances.

།གསུམ་པ་དམིགས་པ་ཏིང་ངེ་འཛིན་གྱི་རྩ་སྐྱོན་བསལ་བ་ནི། ཕྱིར་སེམས་ཀྱི་རྒྱལ་པོ་སྐུ་ཚོགས་སུ་འཕོས་པས། རྒྱུན་ཁྲིད་དེ་རྒྱུན་སེམས་ཡོག་པར་འཇུག་པ་ཡིན་པས་ན། དམིགས་པས་རྟེན་གཅིག་ལ་བཟུང་བས་ལས་སུ་རུང་བར་འགྱུར་བའོ། དེ་ཡང་སྟེ་བའི་ཚོག་སུ་གསུམ་མེ་ཡི་དཀྱིལ་འཁོར་དུ། མཁའ་འགྲོ་མ་འདེགས་བྱེད་སྐྱོལ་མ། ཚད་པ་ཆེ་ན་སྦྱང་ཁྲ། གྲང་བ་ཆེ་ན་དམར་པོ། གྲི་ཁུག་དང་ཐོད་ཁྲག་ཚན། ཐབས་ཀྱི་ངོ་པོ ཁ་ཏོༀ་ཁ་ལ་འབྱུང་པ། དེ་ཡང་དམར་འབར་མེ་ཡི་རང་བཞིན་མོ་ཁབ་ཚམ་ཞིག་ལ་སྐྲ་གཏད་དོ། །རྩ་དྲུ་མའི་ནང་གི་དམིགས་པ་དེ་ཤིན་ཏུ་ཕྲ་ན་དོང་སྐྱེ་སྒྱུར་བ་ཡིན་ནོ། །དེ་ནི་དང་པོའི་དུས་སུ་བཟུང་བར་འགྱུར་རོ། །དེ་ནས་གང་བདེ་ལ་སྦྱོས་ཀྱིན་བྱ་སྟེ། སེམས་བྱིན་ཀྲོང་ཆེ་ན་ཨ་དམར་པོ་ལ་གཏད། རྟོག་པ་མང་ན་ཐིག་ལེ་དཀར་པོ་ལ་གཏད། གྲང་བ་ཆེ་ན་མེ་ཡི་རྒྱན་ལ་གཏད། དེ་ལས་སོགས་པ་གང་བདེ་བ་ལ་སྦྱོས་ཀྱིན་བྱའོ།

།དེ་ནས་ཡེ་ཤེས་རྟེན་ནས་ཐེབ་པ་ཆེན་པོའི་ངོ་བོ་ཉིད་ཀྱི་ངང་ལ་གཏུམ་མོ་བཟུང་བ་ཡིན་ནོ། །དེ་དག་ནི་དམིགས་པས་རྒྱུན་སེམས་དྲུ་མར་འཛུད་པར་བྱའོ། །ཞེས་བྱུང་བས། སྔ་གནད་དང་ཏིང་འཛིན་གཉིས་པོའི་སྦྱང་པ་འདི་སྟར་བཞིན་ཕུན་བཞིར་སྦྱང་པ་དང་། སྐབས་འདིར་ཏིང་འཛིན་གཉིས་པོ་བསྒོམ་ཚུལ་སྦྱང་པ་ཡིན་ཞིང་། སྐབས་སུ་བབས་ཚེ་ལུག་ལེན་ཐབས་པར་བྱེད་དགོས། ཁྱད་པར་དུ་སྟེ་བའི་ཚོག་གི་མེ་ཡི་དཀྱིལ་འཁོར་དུ་དམིགས་པའི་མཁའ་འགྲོ་འཇའ་ཚིག་ལེ་གང་ངོས་པ་དེ་ཞིད་ཡུན་རིང་དང་གསལ་བར་བརྟན་པོར་བྱེད་པ་ཞིན་ཏུ་གལ་ཆེ་བ་ཡིན་པས་འདི་ནས་ནན་གྱིས་བསྒོམ་ཚུལ་དང་། སྐྱོན་ཪོ་ཤེས་པ་དང་དེ་བྱུང་ན་བཅོས་ཤེས་པ་བཅས་ལ་བསྐྱབ་པའོ། །འདི་རྣམས་ཞག་གསུམ་གྱི་བར་དུ་སྦྱང་པའོ། དེ་རྣམས་སྦྱན་འགྲོ་ལུས་འདུལ་ལོ།

Third, as regards elimination of problems of the channels by way of concentration on the visualisation. In general, the king of the mind can project anything, and if due to this instruction on breathing the wind and mind have gone the wrong way, then if you hold (the mind) on one object of visualisation it will become pliable. Focus you mind on *Degdye Drolma* below the navel inside a triangular-shaped mandala of fire. If you are warm she is green-coloured. If you are cold she is red-coloured. She holds a curved knife and skull-cup filled with blood, and embraces a trident that represents the essence of method. She has the nature of blazing fire and the size of a needle. If the visualisation inside the central channel is very subtle the signs of warmth will arise quickly. Maintain this from the beginning. Then change (the object) to what is comfortable. If the mind is excited or drowsy, focus on a red A. If there are too many thoughts focus on a white tigle. If you are too cold, focus on continuity of fire. Focus on whatever is comfortable.

When you have found wisdom, in the state of the essence of the great vehicle, focus on 'inner fire' (*tummo*). These (methods) will make the objects of focus, wind and mind, enter the central channel. As before the training with sound and concentration is done for four sessions per day. At those times, practise meditation with these two types of concentration. When necessary you have to have to apply the practice (to eliminate problems). In particular it is very important to focus clearly, with stability and for a long time on the dakini, the *tigle* or whatever else is suitable in the fire mandala below the navel. Therefore, learn to meditate with insistence, recognize faults and how to (know) how to remedy when they come up. Train like this for three days. This completes the preliminary of controlling the body.

གཉིས་པ་སེམས་འདུལ་གྱི་ཁྲིད་ནི། སེམས་འདུལ་གྱི་ཁྲིད་ལ་གསུམ་སྟེ། འཇམ་རྩུང་
དང་། བར་རྩུང་དང་། དྲག་རྩུང་དོ། །དང་པོ་ལ། ལུས་གནད་བདུན་དང་། དྲག་རྩུང་དགུ་རྣམས་
དང་། དམིགས་པའི་གནད་དང་བོགས་འདོན་འབྱུང་འཁོར་གྱི་གནད་དོ། །

།དང་པོ་ནི།   འདི་ནས་བཟུང་སྟེ་ཕྱུ་ཆུ་རྣམས་ཀྱི་འགྱོར་མཚམས་གཅོད་རྒྱལབས་
སེམས་དགོངས་སྐྱོད་རྣམ་གསུམ། ལུས་གནད་བདུན་དང་། དུག་རྩུང་དགུ་རྣམས་
ཚང་བར་བྱ། དང་པོ་མཚམས་གཅོད་ནི། མ་རྒྱུང་དབང་ཆོག་སྤྲ་བསྒོ་གསང་བ་
གསང་ཆེན་གསང་མཆོག །སོགས་དང་དཔོན་གསས་བླ་མ་སོགས་ལྷུས་དང་།
ཐར་པའི་སྐྱ་ཕུར་སོགས་བསང་དང་། སྐྱབས་འགྲོའི་ཡུལ་བཟློ་ལ། སྟེ་གཉིག་ཁྲ་
གང་སོགས་དང་། ཆོག་བཤད་མཁྲིན་སྤྲ་བརྗེ་བའི་སོགས་དང་། སེམས་བསྐྱེད་ཀྱི་
བསམ་བྱ་ནི། །ཁམས་གསུམ་གྱི་སེམས་ཅན་སོགས་དང་། ཆོག་བཤད་ནི། གསང་བ་
གསང་ཆེན་སོགས་དང་། གསོལ་འདེབས། ཨ་མ་ཡིན་སོགས་དང་། བླ་མའི་དགོངས་
སྟོང་ལ། རྟེན་བསྐྱེད་པ་དང་། མཆལ་འབུལ་བགོ། །དང་པོ་ནི། སེན་ཁྲི་ནི་རྣ་པད་
མའི་གདན་ལ་སོགས་དང་། ཆོག་བཤད། དགོངས་པའི་ཐིག་ལེ་སོགས་དང་། དབང་
སྐྱར། བླ་མའི་སྐུ་གསུང་སོགས་དང་། ཡི་དམ་གྱི་དགོངས་སྐྱོད། ལྷ་བསྐྱེད་པ། རང་གི་
མདུན་གྱི་སོགས་དང་། ཆོགས་འབུལ་ཆོག་བཤད་ནི། གསང་མཆོག་ཡི་དམ་སོགས་
དང་། དབང་བཞི་ལེན་པ། ཡི་དམ་གྱི་སྐུ་གསུང་ཐུགས་སོགས་སོགས་དང་། མཁའ་འགྲོའི་
དགོངས་སྐྱོད་ལྷ་བསྐྱེད། རང་སེམས་སྣོ་ད་སོགས་དང་། ཆོག་བཤད་ནི། རང་སེམས་
རང་ལས་རང་གྲོལ་སོགས་དང་། བྱིན་རྣབས་ཞུ་བ། མཁའ་འགྲོ་མ་ནམ་མཁའ་ནས་
སོགས་དང་།

The method to control the mind

Smooth breathing

There are three practices to subdue the mind: smooth breathing, middle breathing and wrathful breathing. With regards to the first there are key points for the body, key points for breathing, key points for the focus of mind, and key points for magical movements that bring development.

First, from now on at the beginning of each session completely perform setting up of the boundaries, refuge, bodhicitta, the Three States, the seven key points for the body and the nine breathings for purification. First set up the boundaries like in the empowerment ritual of Mother tantra with *'Svo Sangwa Sangchen Sangchog Ku* etc.', then wash with *'Ponse lama etc.'* and purify with smoke with *'Tharpe ke da etc.'.* Then visualise the objects of refuge with *'Chitsug trugang etc.* and sing the verse *'Khyendan Tsewe etc.'.* Then generate the mind of enlightenment with *'kham sum sem chan etc.'* and the verse *'Sangwa sangchog etc.'* Than pray with *'A ma yin etc'.* Then generate the state of the guru and offer mandala by first saying *'Sengtri nyida peme etc.'*, sing the verse *'Gongpe thigle etc.'*, and take initiation with *'Lama ku sung thug etc.'.* Then generate the state of the meditation deity with the words *'Rang gi dun gi etc.'*, offer by singing the verse *'Sangchog yidam gyalpo etc.'*, and take initiation with *'Yidam gi ku sung thug etc.'* Then generate the state of the dakini with the words *'Rang sem OM du gyur etc.'* and take the blessing with *'Namkha ne etc.'*

དེ་ནས་ལུས་གནད་ནི། རྐང་གཉད་དུ་འཇུད་ཕྱིར་ཚིགས་ཕར་འདུག རྡོང་སྐྱེ་སྒྱུར་
ཕྱིར་ཀྲང་པ་གཉིས་བསྒྲིལ། སྐལ་ཚིགས་དྲང་པོར་བསྲང་། ལག་གཉིས་ལྟེ་འོག་གི་
ཐད་དུ་མཉམ་བཞག་བྱ། མགྲིན་པ་ཅུང་ཙམ་བཀུག མིག་གཉིས་སྣ་རྩེའི་ཐད་དུ་
བལྟ། ཚ་རྐྱང་གཉད་དུ་གཟུང་ཕྱིར་དཔུང་པ་ཕྱུང་གཏོག་བཞིན་དུ་གདེངས། རྡོང་
ཏྲགས་སྒྱུར་བའི་ཡན་ལག་ལུས་སེམས་ཐམས་ཅད་རབ་ཏུ་བསྒྲིམས། ཚ་གསུམ་
འབོར་ལོ་ལྟ་རྣམས་གསལ་བ་དང་དངས་ཤིང་ཤོག་ཡངས་པ།

ཚ་གསུམ་གྱི་འདུས་མདོར་མེ་ཡི་ཚ་དབལ་ཅན་གྱི་མཁའ་འགྲོ་མ་ཐུ་མོ་དེ་ལ་
དམིགས་པ་གཏད། དེ་ནས་སྟར་བཤད་པ་བཞིན་དུག་རྐྱང་དགུ་འབུད།

དེ་ནས་བྱེན་རྒྱའི་རྐྱང་སེར་པོ་མགྲིན་པ་བོང་སྟྱོད་ཀྱི་འབོར་ལོའི་གནས་སུ་
དམིགས་པ་བཏན་པོས་བསྟིམ་ཞིང་། རྐྱང་སྟྱོར་ཡན་ལག་བཞི་ཕྲན་ཚང་པར་ཚར་
ལྭ་བཅུ་བྱ། དེ་ཡང་འཇམ་རྐྱང་དུས་རྐྱང་སྟོད་ཀྱི་ཚ་གཅིག་གང་བ་ཚམ་དུ་རྐྱང་
བཟུང་བའི་ཡུན་ཚད་བྱ། དེ་ལྟར་རྐྱང་བཟུང་བཞིན་སྐྱེ་གཡས་གཡོན་དུ་ཐེངས་
གང་འགབ་སྐྲ་ར་ར་གཅུལ་རྐྱང་གཏོང་དུས་ཚངས་བུག་ནས་འཕང་བའི་དམིགས་
པ་བྱ། དེ་ལྟ་བུ་ཉི་མ་རེར་ཐུན་བཞི་རེ་སྟྱོང་བཞིན་ཐུན་མཐར་བསྒོ་སྐོན་བྱ། དེ་ལྟར་
ཉི་མ་ལྔ་བར་གྱིན་རྒྱའི་རྐྱང་སྟྱོང་ངོ་།

Then (apply) the key points for the body (posture): take the rishi position in order to cause the winds to enter at the right place. Cross the legs in order to quickly generate warmth. Straighten the spine. Hold the two hands below the navel in the mudra of meditative balance. Bend the throat slightly. The eyes look straight at the point of the nose. Raise the upper arms like the wings of a garuda bird in order to make the winds and channels enter the correct position. Intensively discipline body and mind with these limbs of practice that quickly generate the signs of warmth.

Focus on the three channels and the five chakra-wheels that are clear, pure and spacious, and on a subtle dakini with hot flames at the junction of the three channels. Then, as explained previously expel the impure air nine times.

Then focus with stability to absorb the yellow upward-voiding wind in the chakra of enjoyment at the throat. Perform the breathing with four stages, fifty times. When practising smooth breathing fill up just one part[11] and hold the wind. While you hold the wind in this way, turn the neck (head) counter-clockwise and clockwise as many times as comfortable. When breathing out, visualise that the wind leaves through the port of Brahma. In this way practice four sessions a day and at the end (of each session) say prayers and the dedication. Practice with the upward voiding wind for five days.

---

11   One part out of three parts, i.e. one third of your breathing capacity.

ཞིན་དུག་པ་ནས་སྒོག་འརྫིན་གྱི་ཕྱན་སྟོང་ལ། སྱར་བཞིན། མཚམས་གཅོད། ཁྲུས་
བསང་། རྒྱབས་སེམས། དགོངས་སྤྱོད་རྣམ་གསུམ། ལུས་གནད་དགུ་དང་ཆ་བརྗེད་
དུག་རྩང་འཐུང་པ་སོགས་སྤྱར་ལྱར་བྱ། །དེ་ནས་ཐུན་རེའི་འགོར་གྱེན་རྒྱ་སོགས་
སྟོན་མའི་དམིགས་པ་དང་འཕུལ་འབོར་རྣམས་བྱུས་པའི་མཐར། དམིགས་པ་སོག་
འརྫིན་གྱི་རྩང་དགར་པོ་སྟེང་ཁ་བོན་ཞིད་ཀྱི་འབོར་ཝོའི་དབུས་སུ་སྤོད་པ་དང་
བསྐྱིས་པ་བྱེད་བཞིན། ལག་གཡས་པས་ཁུ་ཆུར་བཅངས་ནས་ཞགས་པ་འཐེན་པའི་
ཚུལ་དང་། སོར་མོ་རེ་རེ་བཞིན་དགྲོལ་བ་ཐེངས་རེ་བྱ་བ་ལན་ལྔ་དང་། གཡོན་པས་
གྱང་དེ་བཞིན་ལྔ་དང་། རོ་སྤོད་གཡས་སྐྱལ་གཡོན་སྐྱལ་ལྔ་བྱའོ། །ཡན་ལག་བཞི་
ཕུན་གྱི་རྩང་ཁུགས་རེ་རེར་གྱེན་སྒོག་གཞིས་ཀྱི་འཕུལ་འབོར་ཚོན་བ་རེ་བྱ། དེ་ལྱར་
ཞིན་རེར་ཐུན་བཞི་དང་། ཐུན་རེར་རྩང་ཁུགས་ལྔ་བཅུ་རེ་འགྲོ་བར་བྱེད། ཞག་ལྔ་
ཡི་བར་དུ་སྦྱང་བའོ།

From the sixth day, when practising sessions with the life-supporting wind, like before set up of the boundaries, purify by washing and with smoke, take refuge, generate the mind of enlightenment, perform The Three States, take the nine key points for the body, visualise the channels and expel impure air nine times. Then, at the beginning of each session focus on the upward-voiding wind and perform the magical movement as before. Thereafter, while visualising that the white life-supporting wind relaxes and is absorbed in the centre of the chakra of the nature of reality in the heart, throw the right hand fist, like throwing a lasso, and release each finger, five times. Do the same with the left hand. Rotate the right side of upper five times and rotate the left side of the upper body five times. In each breathing cycle with four characteristics, perform the magical movement for both the upward voiding and life sustaining winds. For five days perform four sessions a day and fifty breathing cycles per session.

།དེ་ནས་མེ་དང་མཉམ་པའི་འཕུལ་འབྱོར་ནི། སྤུར་བཞིན་མཆམ་གཙོད། ཁྲུས་
བསང་། རྒྱབས་སེམས། དགོངས་སྦྱོད་ ལུས་གནད་དགུ་དང་རྩ་བསྐྱེད། དུག་རླུང་
འབྱུད་པ་སོགས་སྤྱར་ལྟར་བྱ། དེ་ནས་དམིགས་པ་མེ་དང་མཉམ་པའི་རླུང་དམར་
པོ་རྗེ་བའི་འཕོར་ལོར་བརྫང་ཞིང་ལུས་སྐྱིལ་ཀྱུང་གིས་གསུམ་པ་སྐྲལ་པར་བརྗ་
ཅིང་ལག་པ་གཉིས་ཀྱིས་མེད་པར་འཐུར་ལ་གཡས་སྐོར་ལྷ་གཡོན་སྐོར་ལྷ་རེ་བྱེད།
ཡན་ལག་བཞི་ལྷན་ཀྱི་རླུང་ཁྲགས་རེ་ཡི་རེང་དུ་བྱེན་སྦྱག་མེ་གསུམ་ཀྱི་དམིགས་པ་
དང་འཕུལ་འབྱོར་ཆང་མ་རེ་འགྲོ་བར་བྱེད་པ་ཐེས་ལྷ་བསྲ། ཐུན་སྐོར་གཅིག་གོ
ཞི་མ་རེ་ལ་ཐུན་བཞི་དང་། ཐུན་མཐར་བསྲྟ་སྐྲིན་བྲ། དེ་ལྟར་ཞག་ལྷ་མེ་མཉམ་ཀྱི་
འཕུལ་འབྱོར་རོ།

།དེ་ནས་ཁྲབ་བྱེད་ཀྱི་འཕུལ་འབྱོར་ནི། སྤུར་བཞིན་མཆམ་གཙོད། ཁྲུས་བསང་།
རྒྱབས་སེམས། དགོངས་སྦྱོད་རྣམ་གསུམ། ལུས་གནད་དགུ་དང་། རྩ་བསྐྱེད་དུག་
རླུང་འབྱུད་པ་སོགས་སྤྱར་ལྟར་བྱ། དེ་ནས་རླུང་ཡན་ལག་བཞི་ལྷན་ཞིག་བརྫང་
བའི་དང་ནས་སྤུར་ཀྱི་འཕུལ་འབྱོར་ཀྱེན་སྦྱག་མེ་གསུམ་ཀྱི་དམིགས་པ་དང་འཕུལ་
འབྱོར་བྱུས་པའི་སྟེང་དུ། དམིགས་པ་ཁྲབ་བྱེད་ཀྱི་རླུང་སྤུང་ཁུ་ལུས་སྦྱི་དང་ཡན་
ལག་ལ་བརྙིམ་པ་དང་། འཕུལ་འབྱོར་དབང་པོ་ཡན་ལག་ཐམས་ཅད་ནན་དུ་
བསྐྱིམ་ཞིང་། ལག་པ་གཉིས་ཀྱིས་རེས་མོས་རྩ་རྒྱུས་རྣམས་ལ་ཡར་བྱུག་མར་བྱུག་
ཡན་ལྷ་ལྷ་དང་། མདའ་འགོང་གཞུ་འགོང་དུ་བྱོ། །དེ་ལྟར་དམིགས་པ་དང་
འཕུལ་འབྱོར་བཞི་པོ་རླུང་ཁྲགས་གཅིག་ཏུ་ཆང་བར་བྱེད་པ་ཆོར་ལྷ་བཅུ་ལ་ཐུན་
གཅིག་དང་། ཞི་མ་རེར་ཐུན་བཞི་དང་། ཞིན་ལྷ་དེ་ནི་ཁྲབ་བྱེད་ཀྱི་འཕུལ་འབྱོར་རོ།

Then apply the magical wheel for the fire-equalising wind. As before, set up of the boundaries, purify by washing and with smoke, take refuge, generate the mind of enlightenment, perform The Three States, take the nine key points for the body, visualise the channels and expel foul air nine times. Hold the visualisation of the red fire-equalising wind in the navel chakra and in cross-legged position draw your stomach towards the back[12], your two hands holding the waist, and turn five times counter-clockwise and five times clockwise. For fifty breathing cycles with the four characteristics, perform the magical movement for the upward voiding, life sustaining wind and fire-equalising wind. That constitutes one session. Perform four sessions a day and at the end of each session dedicate and pray. In this way for five days perform the magical movement of fire-equalising wind.

Then apply the magical movement for the pervasive wind. As before, you set up of the boundaries, purify by washing and with smoke, take refuge, generate the mind of enlightenment, perform The Three States, take the nine key points for the body, visualise the channels and expel foul air nine times.

Then, while holding one breathing cycle with the four characteristics perform the visualisation and magical movements of upward voiding, life sustaining and fire-equalising winds, and after that visualise that the green-coloured all-pervading wind pervades the whole body and dissolves in the limbs[13]. For the magical movement contract the senses and limbs and with the hands rub one after the other the channels and muscles upward and downward five times (on each side) and draw a bow. During four sessions per day practise the fourth visualisation and magical movement, fifty times. In this way perform the magical movement for all pervading wind for five days.

---

12   Five times.

13   The all-pervading wind is located in the central channel between navel and secret chakra and pervades the body like sunrays.

།ཡང་དེ་བཞིན་ཐུར་སེལ་གྱི་འཕུལ་འབོར་ནི། སྤར་བཞིན་མཚམས་གཅོད། ཁྲུས་
བསང་། རྒྱབས་སེམས། དགོངས་སྐོང་རྣམ་གསུམ། ཕྱུས་གཤེན་དཀྱུ་དང་། ཙ་བསྐྱེ་
དག་རྐྱང་འཕུལ་པ་སོགས་སྤར་སྤར་བྱ། དེ་ནས་རྐྱང་ཡན་ལག་བཞི་ཕུན་གྱི་དང་
ནས་སྤར་ཞིན་དམིགས་པ་དང་དང་འཕུལ་འབོར་བཞི་ཡི་རྗེས་སུ་ཐུར་སེལ་གྱི་རྐྱང་
སྟོན་པོ་ལྟེ་འོག་གསང་བའི་ཙ་འབོར་ལ་བསྡིམ་ཞིང་། འཕུལ་འབོར་ནི། འོག་སྐྱོ
གཉིས་དབྱེ་བཅུམ་དུ་བྱ་བ་དང་། ལག་པ་གཉིས་ཀྱིས་ཕུས་མོ་གཡས་ལ་འཧྲུས་ཏེ་
ཀེད་པ་འབོར་ལོ་བཞིན་གཡས་སུ་ཐེངས་ལྔ་བསྐོར། ལག་གཉིས་ཀྱི་ཕུས་མོ་གཡོན་
ལ་འཧྲུས་ཏེ་ཀེད་པ་གཡོན་དུ་ཐེངས་ལྔ་བསྐོར། ལག་གཉིས་ཀྱིས་ཕུས་མོ་སོ་སོར་
འཧྲུས་ནས་ཀེད་པ་ཐེངས་ལྔ་བསྐོར་རོ། དེ་ལྟར་འཕུལ་འབོར་ལྔ་དང་དམིགས་པ་
ལྔ་པོ་བཅས་རྐྱང་ཡན་ལག་བཞི་ཕུན་གྱི་ཁྱགས་པ་གཉིས་དུ་ཚོང་བ་ཚར་ལྔ་བཅུ
ལ་ཕུན་གཉིས། ཉིན་གཅིག་ལ་ཕུན་བཞི། ཉིན་ལྔ་རྗེས་མ་མཐྱར་སེལ་གྱི་འཕུལ་
འབོར། དེ་ལྟར་ཞག་མ་ཉེར་ལྔ་འདི་འཇམ་རྒྱང་གི་ཕུན་སྒྲོང་རོ།

Then in similar fashion there is the magical movement for the downward-clearing wind. As before, set up of the boundaries, purify by washing and with smoke, take refuge, generate the mind of enlightenment, perform The Three States, take the nine key points for the body, visualise the channels and expel foul air nine times. Then, during one breathing cycle with the four characteristics perform the four visualisations and magical movements as before, and after that visualise that the blue-coloured downward-clearing wind is absorbed in the secret chakra below the navel. The magical movement is to open and close the two lower doors. Hold the right knee with two hands while you turn the waist counter-clockwise five times. Hold the left knee with two hands while you turn the waist clockwise five times. Hold both knees with your hands while you turn the waist five times. In this way you perform the five visualisations and magical movements while holding one breathing cycle with the four characteristics. Fifty times constitutes one session. Practise four sessions per day. Perform the magical movement for downward-clearing wind for five days. In this way practice smooth breathing for twenty-five days.

།གཉིས་པ་བར་རླུང་ལ། སྦྱོང་ཚུལ་གོ་རིམ་སྦྱར་བཞིན་དུ་བྱེད་ཅིང་། རླུང་བཟུང་
བའི་ཕུན་ཚོད་བར་རླུང་གི་སྐབས་སུ་རླུང་སྦྱོང་གི་སུམ་ཚ་གཉིས་གང་བའི་ཚོད་
དང་། རླུང་ཁུགས་ཀྱི་གྱང་ས་བདུན་ཅུ་དོན་ལྔ་དགོས་པ་ལས་གཞན་གྱི་སྦྱོང་ཚུལ་གྱི་
རྣམ་པ་ཐམས་ཅད་ལྟ་མ་ཇེ་བཞིན་ཡིན། །ཞག་ཉེར་ལྔ་བར་དེ་ལྟར་སྦྱང་པས་ཁྱོན་
ཞག་ལྔ་བཅུ་པའོ། །ཁྱིར་རླུང་སྦྱོང་ནི། སྐྱེན་ཆྱུང་ལས། རླུང་ནང་དུ་དྲང་དུས་ཐུབ་
ཚོད་འཐེན་པ། སྦྱོང་མེད་བྱེད་པ། ཚོལ་མདུད་མནན་པ་གསུམ་གནད་ཡིན། ཕྱི་ལ་
འཐེན་དུས་རོ་སྦྱོང་བསང་པ། ལོག་རླུང་འཐེན་པ། རིག་པ་ལེ་ལོག་ཏུ་གཏང་པ་
གསུམ་གནད་ཡིན་གསུངས། དེ་ལྟར་ཡིད་ལ་འཛིན་པར་བྱེད།

Medium breathing

Second, with regard to medium breathing, the order of practice is the same as before. The measure of the breath we hold is two thirds of capacity. The number of breathing cycles is seventy-five. For the remainder everything is the same as before[14]. If you practise like this for twenty-five days this makes fifty days in total.

In general, the oral transmission says: 'when inhaling, draw in as much as you can, swallow, and press the Adam's apple[15]: these are three key points for inhaling. When exhaling, straighten the upper body, draw up the lower wind, and focus the mind below the navel: these are three key points for exhalation.' Keep this in mind.

14　While holding during medium breathing a flame of fire rises from the dakini. The heat is hundred times stronger than during smooth breathing. Furthermore one holds with more strength, adds one, two, or three times, and performs the magical movement more intensively, in accordance with one's capacity.

15　Swallow and push down while lowering the chin.

གསུམ་པ་ཕུམ་ཆེན་ནས་དུག་རླུང་གི་སྐབས་སུ་སྟོང་ཆུལ་སྟ་མ་བཞིན། མཆམས་
གཅོད། ཕྱུས་བསམ། སྐྱབས་སེམས། དགོངས་སྟོད་རྣམ་གསུམ། ལུས་གནད་དུག་
དང་། ཆ་བསྐྱེད། དུག་རླུང་འབྱུང་བ་སོགས་སྟར་ལྟར་དང་། དེ་ནས་གྱེན་རྒྱུའི་རླུང་
གི་དཀྱིགས་པ་དང་འཕུལ་འབོར་སོགས་ནས་རིམ་བཞིན་རླུང་ཕུའི་བར། རེ་རེ་ལ་
ཞག་ལྟ་རེ་དང་། ཉིན་ཞག་རེར་ཕུན་བཞི་རེ། ཕུན་རེར་རླུང་ཁུགས་བརྒྱ་རེ། རླུང་
ཁུགས་རེའི་ཡུན་ཆད་རླུང་སྟོད་ལྷམ་མེར་གང་བའི་ཆད་དང་། རླུང་ཁུགས་རེ་ལ་
རླུང་སྟོར་ཡང་ལག་བཞི་ཆད་བ་དགོས། ཁྲིད་ཡིག་ཏུ་ལུང་དངས་པ། ཕུམ་ཆེན་གྱི་
ཆད་ནི་སྐྱེན་རྒྱུད་ལས།   སྐྱིལ་ཀྲུང་བཅས་ཏེ་རླུང་བབུང་ནས་ཐབ་ཚོས་ཕུས་མོ་
གཉིས་དང་དཔྱལ་བ་ལ་རེག་ནས་སེན་གོལ་རེ་བཏབ་པའི་ཡུན་ཆད་གཅིག་ཏུ་
བགྲང་པ་སུམ་ཅུ་ཚ་དྲུག་ཕུན་ཆད་ཞུང་བ། བདུན་ཅུ་ཚ་དྲུག་འཕྲིང་བ། བརྒྱ་ཚ་
བརྒྱད་ཆེ་བ་ཞེས་ཕུམ་ཆེན་བཞིན་དོ། ཞེས་པ་བང་འདུག ཁྲིད་གཞན་དུ་ལུང་དོན་
དུ་མ་བསྟས་པ་འདུག་ནའང་། སྐྱབས་འདི་ནི་ལྷགས་གོང་མའི་དགོངས་པ་རེམ་
གཉིས་ཀྱིས་ལམ་རིམ་བསྟབ་པའི་ཐབས་ལྷགས་ཀྱི་རྒྱུད་དོན་གཉན་མ་ཡིན་པའི་
ཆལ་ལོ། །འོན་ཀྱང་ཡུང་དང་བསྟུན་ནས་དཔྱད་པར་མཛོད།

Wrathful breathing

Third, to practise large vase breathing or wrathful breathing, like before set up of the boundaries, purify by washing and with smoke, take refuge, generate the mind of enlightenment, perform The Three States, take the nine key points for the body, visualise the channels, and expel foul air nine times.

Then practise the visualisation and magical movement for the upward-voiding wind and each of the other four winds successively for five days each, during four sessions per day, and for hundred cycles of breathing during each session. The measure of each breath is at full capacity and each breath has to done with the four characteristics of breathing[16].

The Instruction Manual[17] gives a quotation from the oral tradition to measure large vase breathing: 'While holding the breath in cross-legged position, if one touches both knees and the forehead and snaps the fingers, this is counted as one count. Thirty-six counts constitute a short session (of one breathing cycle), seventy-six constitutes a medium length session and hundred and eight constitutes a large session or large vase breath.'

In other instruction manuals there are various (different) interpretations, but here the method of practice is in two stages[18] as it is intended in the high tantras. This is the original meaning of mantra. However, one has to practise this in accordance with one's (capacity) of breath.

---

16 While holding during wrathful breathing the flame of fire from the dakini rises up to the navel.

17 The Instruction Manual is part of the 'Self Arising of the Three Kayas' *(sku gsum rang shar)*.

18 i.e. the two stages are the practice of *tsa lung* with the five root winds and the practice with *tigles*. The idea is that we first learn to control breathing before we practise with *tigles*. In some other traditions *tsa lung* and practise with the *tigles* are combined.

དེ་ལྟར་དྲག་རྐྱང་ལ་ཞག་ཉེར་ལྔ་སྦྱངས་པས་ཁྲིན་འཇམ་རྐྱང་ལ་ཞག་ཉེར་ལྔ་བར་རྐྱང་ལ་ཞག་ཉེར་ལྔ་དྲག་རྐྱང་ལ་ཞག་ཉེར་ལྔ་བཅས་བསྒོམས་ཞག་བདུན་ཅུ་དོན་ལྔ། ལྷར་སྟོར་འགྲོའི་སྐོར་ཞག་བཅུ། འདི་རྣམས་ཀྱི་རིང་བདུན་ཕྲག་རེའི་མཚམས་སུ་འམ་གང་འགབ་ཏུ་ཁྲུས་དང་བཀྲུ་མཉེ་བྱ་བ་དང་། བཟའ་བཏུང་སོགས་ལ་ཁམས་དང་བསྟུན་པ་གལ་ཆེའོ།

།ཏྲགས་ནི་རྒྱུད་འགྲེལ་ལས། དེ་དག་ཀུན་ལ་རྐྱང་བཟུང་བ་དང་འཕྲོ་ལོ་ལྔ་ལ་དམིགས་པ་རེས་མོས་གཏད་པ་དང་། ལུས་སྟོང་གི་ཡན་ལག་དྲུས་གཞིན་དུ་བྱེད་པའོ། །དེས་དང་པོ་ལུས་ལ་དོང་སྟེ། དེ་ནས་སྟང་བ་འཆར་ཏེ། དང་པོ་སྙིག་ལྟ་བུ་འབྱུང་སྟེ། ས་ཡི་རྐྱང་ཞེན་པའོ། །དེ་ནས་དུ་ལྟ་བུ་འབྱུང་སྟེ་ཆུའི་རྐྱང་ཞེན་པའོ། །དེ་ནས་སྲིན་བུ་མེ་ཁྱེར་ལྟ་བུ་འབྱུང་སྟེ་མེའི་རྐྱང་ཞེན་པའོ། །དེ་ནས་མར་མེ་ལྟ་བུ་འབྱུང་སྟེ་རླུང་གི་རྐྱང་གི་ཞེན་པའོ། །དེ་ནས་ནམ་མཁའ་སྤྲིན་དང་བྲལ་བ་ལྟ་བུ་འབྱུང་སྟེ་ནམ་མཁའི་རྐྱང་ཞེན་པའོ། །དེ་ནས་ཡེ་ཤེས་དངོས་སུ་ཐོབ་པ་འབྱུང་སྟེ། ཕྱིར་ས་ལས་ཀྱི་ཏྲགས་ས་ལས་དང་ཐབ་ཀར་ཆོང་པ་འབྱུང་བ་ནི། ཁ་སྒོ་ལ་པ་དང་ཚ་རྐྱང་གཞིས་བསྟོང་པ་ལས་འབྱུང་བའོ།

Practising wrathful breathing for twenty-five days, smooth breathing for twenty-five days, and medium length breathing for twenty-five days, adds up to seventy-five days. Before that one practises the preliminaries for ten days. During all of this, wash the body and take massage once a week or whenever suitable. Food and drink has to be appropriate to your constitution.

The signs are explained in the commentary to the tantra: 'Practise simultaneously the holding of the breath, focussing one by one on the chakras, and the physical exercises. First, the body will generate warmth. Then, visions will arise. First, as a sign of control[19] over the earth-wind, a vision like a mirage will arise. Then, as the sign of control over the water-wind, a vision of smoke will arise. Then, as the sign of control over the fire-wind, a vision of fireflies will arise. Then, as the sign of control over the wind-wind, a vision of a butter lamp will arise. Then, as a sign of control over the space-wind, a vision like a cloudless sky will arise. Then, the actual achievement of wisdom will arise. In general, the signs of the paths and stages come in direct relationship to these paths and stages. They arise from the combination of meditation and *tsa lung* practise.

---

19 Control over the wind means the wind is balanced and enters the central channel.

།ཅུད་དོན་བཞིན་ཐིག་ལེའི་ཆུལ་ནི། །བརྒྱ་དྲུག་ཕྱེད་ཕྱེད་འབྲི་བའི་རྣམ་པ་ཀུན། །གང་ཟུང་བདེ་བ་འཁར་བས་བྱུང་སེམས་འཕེལ། །ཤིན་ཏུ་དྭངས་པས་མི་རྟོག་སྟོང་པའི་ཉམས། །བཅན་ཐབས་བརྒྱོམ་པའི་སྟོབས་ཀྱིས་དབུ་མར་འཇུག །འབྱུང་བཞི་འདུ་བ་འཁྲུགས་ཀྱང་ཉམ་མི་ང་། །སྟན་སྐྱེས་ཡེ་ཤེས་སྟོབས་ཀྱིས་རྣལ་དུ་ཕེབས། ཞེས་གསུངས་པ་ལྟར་ལམ་ཨེ་རྒྱུད་འགྲོལ་དུ་གསལ་བར་མ་བྱུང་བས། དོན མ་ཐུན་དུ་བསམས་ནས་སྐུ་གསུམ་རང་ཤར་གྱི་ཁྲིད་ནང་། ལུང་དངས་པ་ལྟར་སྟོང་པའི་ཆུལ་ནི། མཚམས་གཅོད། ཕྱུང་བསང་། སྐུབས་སེམས། དགོངས་སྟོང་རྣམ གསུམ། ལུས་གནད། རྩ་བསྐྱེད། དྲུག་རྒྱུང་འབྱད་པ་སོགས་སྟར་སྟར་ཆུལ་བཞིན་བྱ དེ་ནས་ལུས་གནད་དེ་ཡི་སྟེང་དུ། རྩ་འཁོར་རྣམས་སྟར་བཞིན་གསལ་བར་བསྒོམ། དེ་ནས་རྒྱུད་སྟྱོར་ཡན་ལག་བཞི་ལྡན་གྱི་དང་ནས། སྟེ་བའི་ལོག་རྩ་གསུམ་འདུས མདོར་སྒྱུ་གསུམ་མི་ཡི་དཀྱིལ་འཁོར་དུ་མཁའ་འགྲོ་མ་འདེགས་ཕྱེད་སྒྱལ་མ དམར་མོ་གྲི་ཐོད་ཅན་དམར་འབར་མེ་ཡི་རང་བཞིན་མོ་ཁབ་ཚམ་ཞིག་ལ་ དམིགས་པ་གཏད་དེ། རྩུང་ཁྱགས་ཡན་ལག་བཞི་ལྡན་སྟན་བརྒྱ་ལ་ཐུན་གཅིག་ཏུ་བྱས པ་ཉིན་གཅིག་ལ་ཐུན་བཞི། དེ་ལྟར་ཉིན་ཟླ་ལ་ནན་ཏན་གྱིས་སྦྱང་ངོ་། །དམིགས པ་དེ་ལ་བྱིང་རྒྱགས་འཕྲོ་ནོད་ཀྱི་སྐྱོན་མེད་པའི་ངང་ནས་གསལ་བར་བྱང་ངོ་།

Practice with the tigles

The way (to practise) with the *tigles* according the (Mother) tantra: 'Sixteen *tigles* decrease to half their number etc.[20] Each (decrease) leads to the arising of bliss and the increase of bodhicitta[21]. As the *tigles* are very pure you will have the experience of non-conceptual emptiness. When by the power of meditation on the forceful method, the *tigles* enter the central channel; you are fearless even when the four constituent elements are disturbed. Through the power of innate wisdom, you rest naturally.'

Because the way to practise is not clearly explained in the commentary and because I[22] think the guide called the 'The Self Arising of the Three Dimensions' is in accordance with the meaning (intended in the root text), I include a quotation from that text: 'The way to practise is like before: set up the boundaries, purify with water and smoke, take refuge, generate the mind of enlightenment, practise the 'Three States', apply the key points for the body, visualise the channels, and expel the foul air. While (holding) the key points for the body, clearly meditate on the five chakras. Then, while performing the breathing with four stages, focus on the visualisation of the red dakini *Degdje Drolma* inside a fire mandala at the junction of the three channels below the navel. She holds a curved knife and a skullcap, has the nature of blazing fire, and is the size of needle. One hundred cycles of breaths with the four stages constitute one session. Practise four sessions a day intensively for five days. Practise the visualisation clearly without faults or agitation.

---

20 While descending sixteen tigles decrease to eight, eight to four, four to two, two to one.

21 I.c. *byang sems* refers to physical drops.

22 i.e. the writer.

།དེ་ནས་སྟོང་འགྲོ་རྣམས་ཚུལ་བཞིན་བྱས་པའི་རྗེས་སུ། ཉེ་བོག་གི་མཁའ་འགྲོའི་མེ་
ཡི་ཚ་དབལ་རྒྱས་ཏེ་སྐྱེ་བོའི་འཁོར་ལོའི་དབུས་སུ་ཉ་ཡིག་དཀར་པོ་མགོ་ཕྱར་དུ་
བསྟན་པ་ལ་མེ་སྟེ་ཕོག་པས་ཉ་ཡིག་ཞུ་ནས་མེ་ནང་དུ་བབས་པ་ལ་དམིགས་ནས་
རླུང་ཁུགས་བཅུད། དེ་ནས་མེ་སྟེ་ཡིས་རྩ་འཁོར་རེ་རེ་པས་ཁེངས་སྟེ་ཐབས་ཤེས་
འཁོར་ལོ་མེ་ཡིས་གང་བ་ལ་དམིགས་ཏེ་རླུང་ཁུགས་ཉི་ཤུ། དེ་བཞིན་དུ་སྐྱེ་བ་སྐྲལ་
བའི་འཁོར་ལོ་མེ་ཡིས་གང་བ་ལ་དམིགས་ཏེ་རླུང་ཁུགས་ཉི་ཤུ། ཕོ་ཉིད་འཁོར་
ལོ་མེ་ཡི་གང་བ་ལ་དམིགས་ཏེ་རླུང་ཁུགས་ཉི་ཤུ། ཕོང་སྟོང་འཁོར་ལོ་མེ་ཡིས་
གང་བ་ལ་དམིགས་ཏེ་རླུང་ཁུགས་ཉི་ཤུ། བདེ་ཆེན་གྱི་འཁོར་ལོ་མེ་ཡིས་ཁེངས་བ་
ལ་དམིགས་ཏེ་རླུང་ཁུགས་ཉི་ཤུ་སྟེ།/ཚ་རླུང་རེ་ལ་རླུང་ཁུགས་ཉི་ཤུ་རེ་གསུངས་
པའི་དོན་ནི་གདུམ་མོའི་མེ་སྐྱེ་ཡར་སྤྲར་བ་ལ་བཀག །ཐིག་ལེ་མར་དབབ་པ་ལ་བཅུ་
རེ་བརྩིས་པའི་ཉི་ཤུ་འགྱུར་བའོ། །མཆན། རླུང་ཁུགས་བཅུ་དང་བཅུད་དེ་ཐུན་
གཅིག ཉིན་རེར་ཐུན་བཞི་དང་། ཐུར་རེར་རླུང་སྟོར་ཡག་ལག་བཞི་སྙེན་བཅུད་དང་
བཅུད་རེ་བྱས་པ་ཉིན་ལྕ་ལ་དེ་སྤར་སྦྱང་།

Then, after having done all the preliminaries, the flames of fire of the dakini below the navel increase and reach the white letter HAM[23] that is upside down in the centre of the crown chakra. During eight breaths visualise that the letter HAM melts and (drops) descend into the fire[24]. Gradually the flames fill up the chakras. For twenty breaths visualise that the chakra of method and wisdom is filled with flames. For twenty breaths visualise that the chakra of manifestation at the navel is filled with flames. For twenty breaths visualise that the chakra of the nature of reality is filled with flames. For twenty breaths visualise that the chakra of enjoyment is filled with flames. For twenty breaths visualise that the chakra of great bliss is filled with flames[25]. Thus, one hundred and eight breaths constitute one session. Practise like this for five days. Practise four sessions every day and during each session practise one hundred and eight breathing cycles with the four stages.

---

23   HAM represents method while the dakini represents wisdom. In some traditions the HAM is visualised inside a *tigle*. But here we visualise just the HAM itself. Because the HAM represents the essence of *tigle* this is sufficient.

24   Literally it reads the HAM melts (*ham yig zhu*). It means the HAM kind of 'sweats'. So the HAM remains in place while drops start to form and fall down into the fire of the dakini.

25   Oral elucidation: wisdom fire goes up through each of the five chakras, one by one, and at each chakra one takes ten cycles of breath. Nectar goes down through five chakras, one by one, and at each chakra one takes ten cycles of breath.

དེ་ལྟར་བསྒོམ་པའི་མི་དགེ་རྟ་ཡིག་བཞུས་ནས་སྐྱེ་བོའི་རྒྱུ་འབྱོར་གང་བའི་ཚེ་ལྷན་སྐྱེས་ཀྱི་དགའ་བ་དང་། དེ་ནས་མགྱིན་པའི་འབྱོར་ལོ་བབས་ལས་ཡས་བབས་ཀྱི་དགའ་བབས་ཁྱད་པར་གྱི་དགའ་བ་ལ་སེམས་བཟུང་། དེ་ནས་ཐིག་ལེ་སྟེང་ཁར་བབས་པས་མཆོག་དགའ་ལ་སེམས་བཟུང་། དེ་ནས་སྟེ་བའི་འབོར་ལོར་བབས་པས་དགའ་བའི་ཁྱད་པར་གྱི་དགའ་བ་ལ་སེམས་བཟུང་། སྟེ་བ་ནས་གསང་བའི་འབོར་ལོར་བབས་པས་དགའ་བའི་ལྷན་སྐྱེས་ཀྱི་དགའ་བ་ལ་སེམས་བཟུང་། དེའི་ཚེ་ལུས་ཐམས་ཅད་བྡེ་རྒྱལ་མར་ཁྱབ་ཞིངས་པ་བཞིན་དུ་བྱང་སེམས་བདུད་རྩིའི་རྒྱུན་གྱིས་གང་བས་བདེ་དྲོད་མེ་མེར་ཆེལ་ཆེལ་སྐྱེས་པར་བསྒོམ། འདིའི་སྐོམ་ཚུལ་རྟེན་མེད་དུ་སྦྱང་བའི་ལུགས་ཡིན་ལ། རྟེན་བཅས་སུ་སྦྱང་བ་དང་། ཐེག་ལེ་དབབ་བསྐྱེག་དགྲམ་པ་སོགས་ནི་རྒྱུད་འདི་ནས་བསྟན་ཀྱང་འགྲེལ་བ་བྱས་པ་མེད་པས་ལ་ལམ་སྡུང་ཐབས་འདི་ཚོར་གྱིས་འཕུས་པར་བྱ། རྒྱལ་ལམ། །ཁ་བཏུད་བཙུ་དྲུག །ཕྱེད་ཕྱེད་ཐིག་ལེ་རྣམས། །དབབ་དང་བསྒོག་དང་བཀག་པའི་ཕུག་རྒྱ་ཡིས། །ཐག །བཅས་ཟག་མེད་བདེ་ཆེན་ལུས་འགྱུར་ནས། །བདེ་གསལ་ས་དང་འཕྱང་པས་ས། །ཚེས་གོམས། །ས་ལས་འདས་པའི་དོན་དུག་དབྱིངས་སྒྲུབ་ནས། །སངས་རྒྱས་མཆོན་འགྱུར་མ་རྒྱུད་པའི་པའི་ལ། །ཀུན་ཏུ་བཟང་མོ་རྒྱུ་ན་འདས་པའི་ཕུལ། །རྣམ་གྲོལ་ཐབ་མོའི་ལས་འདིར་ཞུགས་པར་མཛོད། །ཅེས་གསུངས་པའི་ཕྱིར།

When the letter HAM has been melted by the fire and the crown chakra is filled (with *tigles*), (concentrate on) innate joy. When (the *tigles*) descend to the throat chakra, concentrate your mind on descending joy or special joy. When the *tigles* descend to the heart chakra concentrate your mind on excellent joy. When they descend to the navel chakra concentrate your mind on especially joyous joy. When they descend from the navel to the secret chakra concentrate your mind on innate joy of joy[26]. At this time visualise that the whole the body is filled with a stream of nectar of *tigles*, like filling a leather bag with (liquid) butter. This causes the body to overflow and shine with bliss and inner heat. This is the way to practise without consort.

Though this tantra teaches to practise with a consort in which (*tigles*)[27] descend, return upward and are spread, there is no commentary. Therefore, practise this method (without consort) intensely. The tantra says: 'By way of the practice with a consort all four, eight, and sixteen (*tigles*) descend, return upward[28] and are spread. Thus, the substantial (physical bliss) is transformed into insubstantial great bliss. When you reach the stage of bliss and clarity, familiarise yourself with it. When you achieve the pure dimension with six meanings, beyond the stages (on the path), you have actualised Buddhahood. This is the path of bliss of Mother Tantra. It is the path that Kuntu Zangmo left while going to nirvana. Enter this deep path that liberates everything.'

---

26   In general four joys are mentioned. In this case five joys are mentioned. This is related to union practice in which joy first starts with ordinary joy in the secret chakra. This ordinary joy is not included when counting four joys.

27   Here *tigles* refer to those that are naturally present in the chakras.

28   When practising with a consort joy starts with ordinary joy in the secret chakra and goes up in four stages to the crown chakra where the final innate joy is the actual wisdom of bliss and emptiness. When practising without consort joy starts in the crown chakra and comes down in stages to the secret chakra where it reaches innate joy.

ཕྱགས་སེམས་གཉིས་ཕྱག་ལེ་སྟོང་ཚུལ་ལ་མི་འདུ་བ་ཆེར་མེད་ཀྱང་། སྣང་བའི་
དགོངས་གཞི་དགོས་པ་ཕྱགས་སེམས་གཉིས་མི་འདུ་སྟེ། ཚོགས་ཆེན་གྱིས་ཕྱེད་
འགར་རྟེན་བཅས་ཀྱི་ཕྱག་ལེ་ལ་བརྟེན་ནས་སྣང་བའི་དགོས་པ་ནི། ཁ་སྟོང་ཀྱི་བའི་
བ་མཐར་ཕུག་གི་དོ་བོ་དེ་དྲན་ཆོག་གིས་མ་བསྐྱད་པ། བདེ་སྟོང་གི་རང་བཞིན་སྐུ་
བསམ་བཏོང་མེད་དུ་དོ་སྐྱང་པ་དེ་ཉིད་རང་གི་དོ་བོ་རང་ལ་གསལ་ཞིང་སྟོང་པ་
ཆེན་པོ་ཡུལ་དང་ཡུལ་ཅན་གྱི་བཀད་པ་བྱེད་ས་མེད་པ་དེ་ཉིད་རང་རིག་ཡེ་ཤེས་
སུ་དོ་སྟོང་པའི་ཐབས་སུ་གསུངས། འགྲོ་བ་ཕར་པས་དེ་ལྟ་བུའི་སྟོང་པ་དང་ཚོང་
བ་བྱེད་མོང་ཀྱང་། དེ་ཉིད་དོན་དང་ལྡན་པ་ཡིན་པ་མ་ཤེས་པས་ན་རྒྱངས་ཀྱང་
ཕན་མེད་དོ། །རང་འབྱུང་ཡེ་ཤེས་སེམས་ཅན་ཀུན་ལ་འབྱལ་མེད་དུ་ཡོད་ཀྱང་རོ་
མ་ཤེས་པས་ཕན་མེད་པ་བཞིན་ནོ།

།ཕྱགས་གོང་མས་ཕྱག་ལེ་སྟོང་པའི་དགོས་པ་ནི། དབུ་མའི་ཨ་ཤད་ཀྱི་མེ་ཡིས་ཧྰ་
ཡིག་བཞུས་པའི་ཁུ་བ་ཡས་བབས་དང་མས་ཡར་བརྫོག་པ་སོགས་ལ་བརྟེན་ནས་
དགའ་བཞི་ཆོས་བཟུང་བ་དང་། དེ་མཚུངས་བདེ་སྟོང་གི་རང་བཞིན་ལ་གོམས་པ་
བྱེད་པ་དང་། གོམས་ནས་བདེ་སྟོང་གི་དོ་བོ་དེ་ཉིད་དག་པའི་སྐུ་མའི་ལུས་ཀྱི་རྟེན་
གཞི་བྱེད་པ་དང་། རྟེན་དེ་ལ་མཚོང་སྣོལ་ལས་ཀྱིས་བསྒུལ་པའི་ས་ལས་བགྲོད་པ་
དང་། རིག་འཛིན་གོང་མའི་ཡོན་ཏན་ལ་དབང་བ་སོགས་ཀྱི་ཆེད་ཡིན་པས་ཤེས་
ཏུ་གལ་ཆེའོ། །གཞན་ཡང་དབང་བཞི་པའི་སྐབས་སུ་རྟེན་ཅན་དང་རྟེན་མེད་གང་
རུང་ལ་བརྟེན་ནས་ལས་སྟོར་གྱིས་བདེ་སྟོང་བསྐྱེད་པ་སོགས་གསུངས་པ་དག་ཡེ་
ཤེས་དོ་སྟོང་པའི་ཐབས་སུ་གསུངས་པ་ཡིན་པ་ཤེས་པར་བྱའོ།

Though the way to practise with the *tigles* does not differ much in tantra and dzogchen, the main point and purpose are different. According to some dzogchen manuals the purpose of practising with substantial *tigles* with a consort is (to introduce) the essence of the final bliss of union. This essence is not stained by concepts, it has the nature of bliss and emptiness, and it is beyond words and thoughts. This essence itself is clear to itself, and you cannot identify a subject that knows the object, great emptiness. This is said to be a method of introduction to wisdom awareness. Even though ordinary beings, practice and experience (union), because they do not know it has this quality, it has no benefit. In the same way that, even though all sentient beings have self-arising wisdom without (ever) being separated from it, it has no benefit because they do not recognize it.

According to high tantra[29] the purpose of practising with *tigles* is to:

- Recognize the four joys (that arise) when the heat of the short A in the central channel melts the HAM, and liquid descends downward and returns upward;
- Become familiar with the nature of bliss and emptiness that is similar (to these joys);
- Make the essence of bliss and emptiness into the base for the pure illusory body;
- Travel the paths and stages of seeing and meditation, and
- Achieve the qualities of a knowledge-holder.

Therefore, it is very important. Furthermore, it is said that when at the time of the four initiations bliss and emptiness are generated through practices with or without a consort, this is a method of introduction to wisdom.

---

29 The high tantric vehicles are the vehicle of the white A *(A dkar theg pa)* and the vehicle of the primordial practitioner *(yes shen thegpa)*.

།ཐབས་འདི་རྣམས་ལ་བརྟེན་ནས་དབུ་མའི་རྩ་ལ་ཕྱི་ནས་རྩ་གཡས་གཡོན་ཉང་གི་རྒྱུ་མ་འཇུག་པའི་རླུང་སེམས་ཐམས་ཅད་དབུ་མོའི་རླུང་སེམས་ལ་བསྡུས་ཏེ། ཕྱ་མོའི་རླུང་སེམས་དེ་དག་ནས་དགོས་པའི་ཚེ་དབུ་མ་སོགས་གང་ལ་གཏད་པ་དེར་གནས་པ་འབྱུང་བས། བསྐྱེད་རིམ་གྱི་ལྷ་སྐུ་དབུ་མའི་ཕྱ་མོའི་རླུང་སེམས་ལ་བསྟིམ་ཞེས་པའི་ཚིག་ཏུ་མ་འབྱུང་བ་ཡིན་པས། རླུང་སེམས་ཀྱི་རང་བཞིན་དེ་ལྟར་ཡིན་པ་ཤེས་པར་བྱེད། དེ་ རྗེས་རླུང་སེམས་དག་པའི་རྗེས་སུ་བདེ་སྟོང་གི་རང་བཞིན་གྱི་སྐུ་འགྲུབ་པའི་ཚུལ་དང་། བསྒྲུབ་པའི་ཐབས་རྣམས་རྣམ་པ་འདི་ལ་སྲུངས་ནས་ཤེས་དགོས་པ་དང་། དོན་ཞེས་པར་བསྒྲུབ་པ་དང་། གྲུབ་པར་བྱེད་པའི་ཚུལ་འདི་དང་། སྐྱེ་བ་ལས་ཁྱེར་གྱི་ཁྱིད་རྣམས་ལ་བརྟེན་ནས་གསང་སྔགས་ཐེག་པ་ཆེན་པོའི་རྣལ་ འབྱོར་པ་འམ། སྔགས་པ་ཞེས་བྱ་བ་འབྱུང་ངོ་།

When you have opened the central channel with this method, the gross wind and mind in the left and right channels will dissolve in the subtle wind and mind. The subtle wind and mind will abide wherever[30] you focus in the central channel. The deity that has been generated during the generation stage will dissolve into the subtle wind and mind in the central channel. This is said in many texts. Therefore (first) you have to know the nature of the winds and mind, thereafter you have to purify[31] the wind and mind, and you have to know how to create a body that has the nature of bliss and emptiness thereafter. So, you have to understand the exposition on the method of practice and practise its real meaning (correctly according to its meaning). And (also) you have to know the instruction on how to take dreams onto the path (practice with dreams). Thus, you can be called a yogi (*rnal 'byor pa*) of the great vehicle of secret mantra or ngagpa (*sngags-pa*).

---

30   Wherever means at whichever chakra in the central channel you focus.

31   Here 'to purify' means 'to dissolve' into the central channel. Purification takes place by dissolving winds because than they cease to function as support for disturbing emotions.

།ཐིག་ལེའི་སྤྱོང་ཚུལ་ལ་ཐུགས་ཉམས་གཉིས་མི་འདུ་བ་ཆེར་མེད་ཀྱང་། སྦྱང་བའི་
དགོངས་གཞི་དགོས་པ་ཐུགས་ཉམས་གཉིས་མི་འདུ་སྟེ། ཆོག་ས་ཆེན་ཀྱི་ཡུང་འགའ་
ཞིག་གིས་རྟེན་ཅན་ཀྱི་ཡུལ་ལ་བརྟེན་ནས་ཐིག་ལེ་སྦྱང་སྟེ། དེ་ཡང་ཁ་སྤྱོར་ཀྱི་བདེ་
བ་མཐར་ཐུག་གི་ངོ་བོ་དེ་བསམ་དྲན་ཚིག་པ་མེད་པ། བློ་ཚིག་གིས་མ་བསྐྱེད་པ།
བདེ་སྤྱོང་གི་རང་བཞིན་དེ་སྐྱེ་མི་བཏུབ་པ། རང་གི་ངོ་བོ་རང་ལ་གསལ་བ་ལས་
གཞན་ཀྱི་ཡུལ་ཅན་གང་གི་ཡུལ་མ་ཡིན་པ། དེ་ཉིད་གནས་ལུགས་བདེ་སྤྱོང་ཡེ་
ཤེས་སུ་ངོས་བཟུང་ངོ་སྦྱང་། དེ་ལྟར་ངོས་བཟུང་བའི་ཚུལ་དེ་ལ་གོམས་པ་བསྐྱེད་
པའོ།

།ཐུགས་གོང་མའི་ལུགས་ཀྱི་ཁ་སྤྱོར་ཀྱི་བདེ་སྤྱོང་གི་རང་བཞིན་བསམ་བརྗོད་ལས་
འདས་པ་དེ་ཉིད་ཀྱིས་ཟག་བཅས་ཀྱིས་བསྒྲུབས་པའི་རྣང་སེམས་སོགས་བདེ་སྤྱོང་གི་
ངོ་བོར་བསྒྱུར་བའི་བདེ་སྤྱོང་དེ་ཉིད་ཆོགས་རིམ་ཀྱི་ལྷ་སྐུའི་རྟེན་དུ་བྱེད་ཀྱང་། ཚོ
དབང་སོགས་རིག་འཛིན་ཀྱི་སྐུ་ཡི་ངོ་བོར་གྱུར་པ། ས་ལམ་སྒྲུབ་པ་པོ་ཡི་རྣལ་
འབྱོར་ཀྱི་རྟེན་ཡིན་ནོ།

Though the difference between the way of practice with *tigles* in tantra and dzogchen is not big, the main point and purpose are different. According to some dzogchen texts the purpose of practising with *tigles* with a consort is that the essence of the final bliss of union is non-conceptual, not stained by any thought.'It is not possible to express this nature of bliss and emptiness in words. Its own essence is clear to itself. Beyond that there is no subject that knows an object. This very nature is the introduction to recognize the natural state of the wisdom of bliss and emptiness. Develop familiarity with this way of recognition.

In high tantra union has the nature of bliss and emptiness, inconceivable and inexpressible. It changes the substantial physical wind and mind into the essence of bliss and emptiness. This is the basis for the body of the deity of the perfection stage. It has the essence of the bodies of a knowledge-holder such as the one with power over life. It is the basis for realisation of the paths and stages by a yogi[32].

---

32   i.e. the four stages of knowledge holders.

།ཚ་དང་རླུང་གི་རྣམ་པ་སྤྱངས་པ་ཡིས། །མདོག་དབྱིབས་ཆད་དང་ཐོད་བཀལ་སྟང་བ་འགགས། །འདུ་བ་འཆར་ཡང་རྒྱུ་དང་དགོངས་གཞི་དག །མཆོངས་མིན་དེ་དག ཚ་རླུང་གནད་འཁྱུན་ཏུགས། །དུ་བ་སྤྲིག་སྨུ་སོགས་ཀྱི་ཏུགས་བཞིན་ནོ། །ཐོད་བཀལ་སྟང་བས་སྲིད་པ་དབང་བསྒྱུར་ཏེ། །ཡེ་ཤེས་འོད་གསལ་དང་དུ་ཕྱག་རྒྱས བཏབ། །འཁར་ཡུས་འོད་ཀྱི་སྐུ་ཞེས་ཟད་མཐར་བསྐྱལ།

།སྤྱགས་ཀྱི་གཞུང་བཞིན་ཚ་རླུང་ཐིག་ལེ་ཡི། །ཕྱག་ལེན་ལ་བརྟེན་ཚ་རླུང་ཐིག་ལེ་སོགས། །རང་སར་གནད་དུ་འཁྱུན་པའི་ཏུགས་ཁར་བ། །དུ་བ་སྤྲིག་སྨུ་སོགས་ཀྱི་ཏུགས་བྱུང་བཞིན། །ཐིག་ལེའི་ཆད་དབྱིབས་མདོག་སོགས་གསལ་སྟང་བ། །ཡེ་ཤེས་འོད་གསལ་སྟང་བ་ཡིན་ཀློམ་ན། །རྒྱུད་དོན་མ་རྟོགས་ནོར་བ་ཆེན་པོའོ། །དེ་བཞིན དབང་ཕྱུག་གྲུབ་མཐའི་ལྟ་བ་ཡི། །ཞད་གསལ་སྟང་བའི་འཆར་ཚུལ་དུ་མ་འགག། །འོད་གསལ་རང་བཞིན་ཀློམ་པའང་སྟང་བས་ན། །བསོད་ནམས་འཕེལ་དུས་སྐུ བསམ་ཇེ་སྲེད་སྟང་། །ཐོད་བཀལ་སྟང་བ་ཡེ་གའི་བསྒོམས་གོམས་ནས། །རང གཞིས་ཡོན་ཏན་མཚོན་པར་སྟང་བ་ཡིན། །ཚ་རླུང་ཐིག་ལེས་བྱས་པ་མ་ཡིན་ནོ། །དབྱིབས་མདོག་མཆོངས་ཀྱང་རྒྱུ་ཀྱེན་ཏོ་བོ་མིན།

Through practice with the channels and winds all kinds of visions of colour and form will arise that are similar to *thogal* visions. Though their appearance is similar (to *thogal* visions) they are different because their cause and the main point are different. These visions are signs of having gained control over[33] the channels and winds, for instance like the signs of smoke and a mirage etc. *Thogal* vision (on the other hand) overpowers (karmic) existence, seals it in the state of clear light wisdom. *Thogal* vision will lead to final exhaustion into what is called the rainbow body of light.

When one practises with the channels, winds and *tigles* in accordance with tantric texts, the signs of naturally gaining control over the channels, winds and *tigles* will appear. In the same way that signs of smoke and mirage etc. appear, all kinds of *tigles*, forms and colours will appear clearly. If you mistake these to be clear light wisdom this is a big mistake of not understanding the meaning of tantra.

Likewise, in the view of the tenets of Maheshvara there are various inner clear visions. When these (visions) are mistaken to be natural clear light it is (a sign of) the time when merit has declined.

When one is familiar with *thogal* visions, while meditating on the primordial base, the visions are of the quality of one's own nature. They are not created by (practising with) channels, winds and *tigles*. Though their form and colour are similar (to visions caused by gaining control over channels, winds and *tigles*) these visions are without cause and condition.

---

33   *gnad 'chun* translated as 'gain control over' means that the winds have entered the central channel.

།ལམ་འདི་རྣམས་བསྒྲུབ་པ་ལ། གེགས་བྱུང་བ་བཅོས་ཤེས་དགོས་ཏེ། རྒྱུད་འགྲེལ་
ལས། དེ་ལྟར་གསང་སྔགས་ཀྱི་རྩ་བ་ཐེག་པ་ཆེན་པོ་བསྐྱེད་པ་ལ། ཡང་དག་པའི་
གནད་རྒྱུ་གིས་ལས་ཐམས་ཅད་བྱེད་པ་ཡིན་པས། གང་ཟག་གི་ཕྱུང་པོའི་ཁམས་
དང་འབྱུང་བ་མི་གཅིག་པས། ནད་དང་གེགས་དང་སྐྱོན་བྱུང་ན་བཅོས་དགོས་པ་
ཡིན་པས། དེ་ལ་ཡང་བསྒྲམ་ན་གསུམ་སྟེ་ཕྱི་ལྟར་དམིགས་པའི་ཐབས་ལམ་གྱིས་
གདོན་སྟོང་ཐག་བཅད་ཅུ་ཞི་བར་བྱ་བ་དང་། ནང་ལྟར་སྤྱང་པའི་ཐབས་ལམ་གྱིས་
ནད་བཞི་བརྒྱུ་ཚ་བཞི་ཞི་བར་བྱ་བ་དང་། གསང་བ་ལྟར་རྟོགས་པའི་ཐབས་ལམ་
གྱིས་ཆོན་མོངས་པ་བརྒྱུད་ཁྲི་བཞི་སྟོང་ཞི་བར་བྱ་བའོ།

དེ་ཡང་གདོན་ཐོག་ཏུ་བབས་པ་འདིའི་ཡི་ཚ་འཕྲུལ་སྐུ་ཚོགས་འཁྲུག་པ་ལ། གདོན་
ཐིས་པར་སངས་རྒྱས་ཀྱི་སྤྲུལ་པ་ཡིན་པས། རང་ལ་བཙོན་འགྲུས་ཀྱི་ཤུག་བྱེད་པའི་
དོན་ཡིན་པས། བྱམས་སྙིང་རྗེ་དང་སྟོང་ཉིད་བསྒོམ་པའོ།

How to eliminate obstacles

Practitioners of this path have to know how to overcome (cure) obstacles that (may) arise. The commentary on the tantra says: 'For those who meditate in this way on the root (practice) of the great vehicle of secret mantra, the pure key point is that everything is a function of the application of the winds. But because the constitution and elements of individuals are not the same, they (may) have to cure (different) illnesses, obstacles, and mistakes. In summary there are three ways (to pacify obstacles): externally one pacifies eighty-four thousand spirits by the visualisation of the path of method[34]. Internally one pacifies four hundred and four illnesses by the practice of the path of method[35]. Secretly one pacifies eighty-four thousand disturbing emotions by the realisation (acquired through) the path of method.

When spirits befall us, we will be disturbed by various apparitions caused by these spirits. As it is sure that these are manifestations of the Buddha, like a whip that incites our joyful effort, (we should) meditate on love, compassion and emptiness.

---

34   i.e. by visualising oneself as Degdje Drolma inside a protective tent of fire.

35   i.e. by practising *tsa lung*.

།ནད་བཞི་བརྒྱ་རྩ་བཞི་ཡོད་ཀྱང་སྐྱོམ་པའི་གང་ཟག་ལ་རྩ་བའི་གེགས་བཅུ་དྲུག་ཏུ
འབྱུང་བ་ཡིན་ནོ། །དེ་གང་ཞེ་ན། འགགས་པ། འཐིམ་པ། རེང་པ། ཤུགས་པ། འབྱམས་པ།
དེད་པ། མགོ་འཐེབ། སྟེང་རྔུང་། སྟོད་རྒྱས། འཕར་འདར། རྒྱུ་འཁྱགས། ཤ་གས་ཁྲག་གསུས
ནད། གཞུང་ནད། ཀེ་རྒྱས། སྐྱ་ཐབ་དང་། ནད་ཀྱི་རིགས་སུ་གྱུར་པ་དང་དེ་ཚོའོ།

།རྒྱུ་གི་ནད་དུ་གྱུར་པ་ཕྱི་རྒྱུད་ལུས་ལ་རེངས་པ། ནད་རྒྱུ་རྩ་ལ་རེངས་པ། གསང་
རྒྱུད་སེམས་ལ་རེངས་པ་གསུམ་གྱིས་བསྒྲབས་པ་རྣམས་སོ། །ཉོན་མོངས་པ་ལས་གྱུར
པ་དེད་ཀྱི་རྣམ་པ་བཞིནོ།

Though there are four hundred and four diseases, for a meditator sixteen basic obstacles may arise. What are these? Blockage, dissipation, rigidity, (winds) entering (the wrong channels), being scattered, roughness, dullness in the head, heart wind, swelling of the upper body, trembling, disturbed sinews, dropsy (oedema) of the flesh, dropsy of the belly, spinal disease, swelling of the waist, and oedema. These are the types of disease.

In summary there are three types of wind disease: disease of outer winds (causes) physical rigidity, disease of inner winds (causes) rigidity of channels, and disease of secret winds (causes) mental rigidity. Four types of roughness come forth from disturbing emotions.

།དེ་ལྟར་སྐྱོན་བཅས་ཞིང་ཡོན་ཏན་བསྐྱེད་པའི་ཐབས་བསྟན་པ་ནི། །འགག་པ་ལ་
གསུམ་སྟེ། རྩུང་འགགས་པ་དང་། དི་ཆེན་འགགས་པ་དང་། དི་རྒྱུ་འགགས་པའོ། །དང་པོ་
ནི། མཁའ་འགྲོའི་གནད་ཀྱིས། རྩུང་ཕྱིར་སོང་། ནང་དུ་མ་འདུས་ནས་འགགས་ན།
ཤུག་མའི་རྩུང་ཕུབ་ཆོད་དུ་མནན་ཞིང་ནང་དུ་བཟུང་ངོ་། །ནང་རྩུང་ཕྱིར་མི་རྒྱུ་
བར་འགགས་ན་སྟ་ཐུག་གཉིས་ནས་དྲག་ཏུ་འབུད། དེ་ལྟར་ཐུས་པས་ཐབ་ནོ། །དི་
ཆེན་འགག་ན་སྟེགས་གཉིས་ཞིང་གཅིག་བཞལ་ལ་གོས་སྟན་གྱིས་སྟིབས་ཏེ། སྟེ་བ་
ཞིང་ལ་བགལ་ལ་ལ་སྐྲབ་འུར་ནས་བྱ་སྟིང་བ་བཞིན་འཁྱུལ་འགྱོར་བྱ། ཀྱང་ལག་
ཡར་མར་དུ་ཤད་ཤད་བརྒྱང་ངོ་། །དི་རྒྱུ་འགགས་ན་ལག་པའི་མཐེབ་ཆེན་གཉིས་
ཀྱིས་དཔྱི་སྟ་གཉིས་ནོན་པར་བྱ། སོར་མོ་གཞན་རྣམས་ཀྱིས་འཕལ་བྱུའི་རྩ་བ་
མནན་ཞིང་བྱུག་ལ། སྤྱིའུ་རྩེ་མཁན་ས་བྱུའི་འཁྱུལ་འགྱོར་བྱའོ། །སྟིང་འགགས་ན་
འོག་སྒོ་གཉིས་བསྐམས་ལ་རྩུང་དང་ཤེས་པ་གཉིས་ཀ་ཀྱིན་ལ་འདོན།
འོག་འགགས་ན་སྟིང་བསྐམས་ལ་རྒྱུ་འོག་ཏུ་གཏད་ལ་ཤད་ཀྱིས་བཏང་ངོ་།

With regard to the teaching on how to correct faults and how to generate qualities, there are three types of blockage: blockage of the winds (breathing), constipation, and blockage of urine.

As to the first:

- In case due to (practising) the key points of the dakini the wind has gone outside and cannot be gathered inside, press the remaining wind as much as you can and hold it inside. When the wind is blocked inside and cannot move out, expel it strongly from the two nostrils. If you do this it will be of benefit.
- In case of constipation put a piece of wood on two supports, cover it as your seat. Lie with your face down, with the navel on the wood, and make the magical movement of a bird hovering about while you stretch out the arms and legs and bring them up and down.
- In case urine is blocked, press the tip of the hips with the two thumbs while the other fingers press and rub the root of the fruit[36]. Meanwhile make the magical movement of a playing monkey.
- In case (wind) is blocked in the upper part of the body restrain (close) the two lower doors and expel wind and mind upward. In case (wind) is blocked in the lower part of the body restrain the upper part, concentrate the wind below and send it out straight out.

---

36   Male or female organ.

།གཉིས་པ་འབྲི་བ་ལ། སྟོད་འབྲིས་སྨད་འབྲི་གཉིས། ཕྱི་འབྲི་ནང་འབྲི་
གཉིས། སྟོད་ཀྲུང་འབྲི་པས་རོ་སྟོད་གཉེར་ཞིང་ཕོ་ཁ་འགས་པ་བྱུང་ན། ཀྲུང་དུག་
ཏུ་བཟུང་ལ་སེང་གེ་སྒྲུག་སྟེབ་ཀྱི་འབྲུལ་འབོར་ལག་པ་གཉིས་གཡས་སྒྱུག་གཡོན་
སྒྱུག་བྱའོ། །སྨད་འབྲིས་སྟོན་ན་ན་ས་མན་ཆད་དུ་ཤེས་པ་གཏད་ལ་གཡག་རྟོ་ཆད་
པའི་འཁྱལ་འབོར་བྱ། །བསྐོམ་བཞག་པའི་དུས་སུ་ཏུ་ཏུ་དྲུག་ཏུ་བྱའོ། ཕྱི་འབྲིས་ཕྱི་
ར་ཀྲུང་འཐུམ་པས། སྨྲ་མ་ཤེས་ན་སྨྲི་བར་ཀྲུང་བཏོན། འགྲོ་མ་ཤེས་ན་ཀྱང་མཐིལ་
དུ་ཀྲུང་བཏོན། གར་ན་ས་ཏུ་སྟོང་པ་དང་ཐྲོལ་ཆག་ལྟ་བུ་བ། ན་བ་ཐོག་དབབ་ཀྱི་
འཁྱུལ་འབོར། ན་ས་ཀུན་ཏུ་མི་གྲགས་པར་བཏུང་ངོ་། །ནང་འབྲིས་ན་མཐོང་བར་
དུ་ཀྲུང་ཞུགས་ནས་སྣྲུ་སྲངས་སུ་སོང་ན། །ན་ས་བོར་ཆོས་བཟུགས་ན་ས་ལག་ཡས་
གཡོབ་ཉིང་བཟུང་པ་ཁྱག་ཁྱག་བྱས་ན་ཕན་ནོ། རུས་མིག་ཐྲ་ཆོའམ་ཀོར་ཆོར་ཀྲུང་
འབྲིས་པས། ཕྱུས་སྣ་གཟེར་ན་ཆ་བྱུང་། གང་ན་ས་ཡི་ཐང་དུ་བད་མ་སྟེ་བའི་
གསང་སུ་ཆན་དུ། ཏུ་སྟོབས་པོ་ཆེས་ནད་ཆུར་ཆུར་འཐེན་པར་བསམས་པས་ཕན་ནོ།

Second, there are upper, lower, outer and inner dissipation:

- When the winds dissipate upward you will have pain in the upper part of the body and the entrance of the stomach will be blocked. Hold the wind firmly and make the magical movement of the lion, alternately shaking the right and left arm.
- When the winds dissipate downward and you are bloated, focus your mind below the spot that is painful and make the magical movement of an exhausted wild yak. When you leave your meditation say HA HA fiercely.
- When the winds dissipate outside of the body your mind will be unclear. If you can't speak, exhale the wind from the throat. If you can't walk, exhale the wind from the soles of the feet. Wherever it hurts, consider this spot to be empty like a sieve. Perform the magical movement of softy beating all painful places.
- When winds dissipate inside the body they enter between visible flesh (i.e. between skin and flesh) and your flesh will become uneven. It will of benefit to pinch the painful area with your fingers, move your hands above it, and beat it with a cupped hand.
- When the winds dissipate in the small concave joints or in the flat round part of the joints, the body will be dry, painful and you will feel ill. It will of benefit to visualise a lotus at the place where it hurts. In its centre there is a secret place with a powerful HAM on top that draws out the illness entirely.

།གསུམ་པ་རེན་པ་ལ་ཡང་གཉིས་ཏེ། དྲག་ཐལ་བས་རེན་པ་སྐྱོ་ཐུང་རེག་པ་སྐྱན་འཆོག་པ་ཟ་བདོ། ཌེ་ལ་ནི་ཆུང་ཟད་སྐྲོད་ཅིང་ལས་དཀར་ཧྱལ་ཐོན་པ་ཚམ་དང་། སྐྲ་གནད་ཀྱིས་སྤྱར་བདོ། །ཞིན་ཐལ་བས་རེན་པ་ལེ་ལོའི་དབང་གིས་བསྐོས་ཆོར་ ཐབས་སུ་སོང་བས། ངན་ལང་དུ་རེངས་ནས་འཇུག་དཀའ་ཞིང་རེན་པདོ། །ཌེ་ལ་ ནི་ལྱས་སེམས་དྲག་ཏུ་གཙུན་ལ་གཏན་འབངས་སུ་མི་བཏང་ལ་བསྐོམ་པདོ།

།ལྱགས་པ་ནི་ཁྱབ་བྱེད་ཀྱི་རླུང་མི་འདོད་པའི་ཕྱོགས་སུ་ལྱགས་པས་ལྱས་འགྱེལ་ ཞིང་འགྲོ་བ་སྟེ། ཌེ་ལ་ཐིག་ལེ་ལ་སེམས་གཏད་པས་བསྲང་བ་ནི། གཡོན་དུ་འགྱེལ་ ན་གཡས་ཀྱི་ཐེའུ་ཆུང་དུ་ཐིག་ལེ་དཀར་པོ་གཅིག་བསམ། གཡས་སུ་འགྱེལ་ན་ གཡོན་གྱི་ཐེའུ་ཆུང་དུ་ཐིག་ལེ་གཅིག་བསམ། མདུན་དུ་འགྱེལ་ན་རྒྱབ་ཀྱི་ལྱག་ཁྲང་ དུ་བསམ། རྒྱབ་ཏུ་འགྱེལ་ན་མདུན་གྱི་དཔལ་བ་ར་དུ་བསམ། ཌེ་ནི་ལེ་ནེས་བཞིའི་ ཐིག་ལེ་བཏབ་པས་སྐྱོང་པདོ།

Third are two kinds rigidity[37]:

- Rigidity that is the consequence of too intensive (practice leads to) a short temper and getting angry with one's relatives. To remedy this, relax a bit, engage in positive physical activities that make you sweat, and practice the key points to elevate with sound.
- Rigidity that is the consequence of too slack (practice leads you) to loose your meditation and to develop a bad habit due to which it will difficult to engage (in practice). To remedy this, exert body and mind intensively and do not let (rigidity) raise its head.

With regard to entering, when the pervasive wind enters in an unwanted direction (i.e. the wrong channel), the body will faint and move. You can rectify this by focussing the mind on a *tigle*. If you faint towards the left side visualise a white *tigle* in the small channel (at the right jaw)[38]. If you faint towards the right side visualise a *tigle* in the small channel (at the left jaw). If you faint towards the front visualise it in the hole at the back of the neck. And if you faint towards the back visualise it at the forehead. This is how to rectify with the four wisdom *tigles*.

---

37 *Ren pa* has the connotation of not tamed, not trained.
38 This channel runs close to the ear.

།ཞུགས་པ་འབྲིང་པོ་འཁྱལ་བའི་རྟར་རྐྱང་སེམས་ཞུགས་གནས་འབོག་བཀྱལ་དུ་
སོང་ན། དེ་དགག་པའི་བསྒོམ་ཐབས་ནི། རྟ་དཔྱ་མ་དང་སེང་དེ་བ་སྟ་ལྟག་ཤུག་ཚམ་
གཞིག་བསམས་པའི་སྟེང་དུ་ཨ་དཀར་པོ་བར་དུ་ཨོྃ་དམར་པོ་མར་སྟེར་ཀྟུ་མཐིང་ཁ།
དེ་གསུམ་རེ་རེ་ལ་ཡང་རང་འདུའི་ཡི་གེ་གྲངས་མེད་པས་གཡས་སྐོར་དུ་བསྐོར་བ་
ལ། བོད་རེར་གྱི་རྒྱུན་དུ་མར་ཡར་འགྲོ་མར་འགྲོ་ཐྱེད་པར་བསམ་ཞིང་། ཨ་ཨོྃ་ཀྟུ་
ཞེས་བཟླས་པ་དང་བསྒོམས་པས་སེལ་བར་འགྱུར། ཡང་ན་རྩ་གཡས་དཀར་དུ་ཨོྃ
གཡོན་དམར་དུ་ཀྟུ། དབུས་མཐིང་དུ་ཨ་ཡིག་ཐམ་མེ་གང་ན་བ་ལ། བོད་རེར་འདུ
འཕྲོ་དཔག་ཏུ་མེད་པ་བསམ་ཞིང་བསྒོམ་པས། དུག་གསུམ་ཞི་ཞིང་སྟུང་བའི་
མཚོག་ཏུ་འགྱུར་རོ།

In middling entering the wind and mind enter the channel of confusion[39]. You go crazy or faint. The meditation method to stop this is to visualise the central channel, immaculately pure, the size of a bamboo whip, with a white A above it, a red OM in the middle, and a blue HUM at the bottom. The three letters are each surrounded by letters that make the same sound (as the A, OM, and HUM) and that turn anti-clockwise. A stream of light rays goes up in the central channel. You meditate like this while reciting A OM HUM and thus eliminate the problem.

Or, think and meditate that the white right channel is completely filled with OM, the left red channel with HUM, and the blue central channel with A. Imagine that immeasurable light rays are emitted and reabsorbed and this pacifies the three poisons and provides superior protection.

---

39 Located at the heart.

།ཞུགས་པ་ཆེན་པོ་ནི་རྩ་སྣ་བསམ་རྩེ་དུག་གི་ནང་དུ་རྐྱང་སེམས་འདུས་པས།
སེམས་ལ་ཅི་བསམ་རྣ་བར་ཏོལ་ཏོལ་གཏུམ་པ་འབྱུང་སྟེ། མི་གཞན་གྱིས་ཅི་བསམ་
པ་གཏུམ་པ་དང་། འདི་རང་ལ་གང་གནོད་པ་ལྟོ་བ་དང་། གཏེར་དང་འཕྲུ་ནོར་
གར་ཡོད་བསམ་ན་དེ་ན་ཡོད་ཟེར་བ་ལས་སོགས་མཆོན་པར་ཤེས་པ་སྟོན་པ་
བཞིན་དུ། རང་ཁ་དང་རང་སེམས་ལྟོ་གྲོས་འགྲིག་པའི་གཏུམ་བརྟོ་བ་འབྱུང་ངོ་།
ཏེ་མ་བཙོས་ན་རྗེ་ཆེ་ལ་བདུད་དང་བསྟོ་འཕོགས་སུ་གྱུར་བས། རྩ་དབུ་མའི་ཡར་
སྙེ་ལ་སེང་ཁྲི་པད་རྒྱའི་སྟེང་དུ་ཡི་དམ་དང་བརྒྱུད་པ་ཐམས་ཅད་གཞན་ཆོན་གྱི་
ཏོད་རྒྱུད་ལ་བསམ་ལ། རྩ་ཁ་ཏོ་ལ་གཏད་པས། བླ་མ་ཡི་དམ་ཏོད་དུ་ཞུ་ནས་རིམ་
པར་བསྟིམ་པས། ཏོ་ལ་བདུད་རྩེའི་རྒྱུན་བབས་ནས་རྩ་ཐམས་ཅད་གང་བར་
བསམ་ཞིང་བསྒོམ་མོ། དེས་སེལ་བར་འགྱུར་རོ།

In big entering, wind and mind gather in the channel of speech and thinking like nectar and poison[40]. You will be clairvoyant like a Buddha and whatever people think will enter your ears: you can tell what people think, what kind of harm spirits inflict, and where there are treasures, wealth and grains. And you will talk to yourself. If you do not correct this it will increase and develop into (possession by) demons and craziness. At the top of the central channel inside rainbow light visualise the meditation deity on top of a lion-throne, lotus and moon[41], together with (the lamas of) the lineage. Focus on the HAM at the opening of the channel. The lamas and the meditation deity melt into light and dissolve one by one. Visualise that from the HAM a stream of nectar descends and fills all your channels. This eliminates (the problem).

---

40   Refers to the life channel *(srog rtsa)*, the channel where the life sustaining wind dwells.

41   Though the text does not mention it there is a sun seat as well.

།འབྲམས་པ་ལ་གསུམ་སྟེ། ཆོག་པའི་སྒྲ་འབྲམས། འབྱུང་བའི་རྒྱུ་འབྲམས། བདུད་ཀྱིས་བྱིན་འབྲམས་པའོ། །དང་པོ་ནི་སེམས་གནས་སུ་མི་འདོད་པར་ཆོག་པ་ལྟ་ཚོགས་སུ་འཕྲོ་བའོ། །དེ་ཡང་རང་གི་ལུས་དང་ཡོ་བྱད་འབགའ་ཞིག་རྒྱུ་ཞིང་འཕྲོན། མདུན་གྱི་ནམ་མཁའ་ལ་སྣ་མ་བསྒོམ་ལ་རང་གི་མགོ་བཅད་ལ་ཕུལ་བས་བཞེས་པར་བསམ། དེ་བཞིན་ཡན་ལག་མགོ་སྟེང་ 〈སྒྲ་སྟེང་〉 ཀུན་ཕུལ་བས་སྟོང་པ་ལ་སྦྱང་ངོ་། །དོན་མེད་པའི་དན་པ་ལྟ་ཚོགས་སུ་འཕྲོ་ན། རྩ་དབུ་མ་གསལ་བའི་འབོར་ལོ་ལྟ་ལ་སྣ་མ་མཚོན་དང་གཟེ་བརྟེད་ལྷན་པར་བསྐྱེད་ལ། ཚོད་ཟེར་ཕྱུང་པོ་ཕྱ་ཕྱ་རམ་རམ་ཤུག་ཤུག་པ་མང་པོས་རྩ་གནས་ཁྱབ་ཅིང་ཁང་པ་མགྲོན་ཀྱིས་གང་བཞིན་དུ་བསམས་མོ། །ཡང་ཤེས་པ་འཁད་ཅིང་འཕྲོ་སྟོང་མི་ཆུགས་པར་འཚོང་པ་ཟ་ན། རྐུང་ཡིན་ཁ་སས་འཚོགས་གསང་དང་རྐུང་གསང་དུ་མི་ཚོལ་དང་བཀག་ཁྲུ་བྱའོ།

There are three types of scattering: caused by the thinking mind, by the dominant element, and by the influence of demons.

In the first case the mind cannot stay put and all sorts of thoughts proliferate:

- If they move and proliferate due to the body and possessions, visualise your lama in the sky in front, cut off your own head and offer it. Consider the lama accepts it. Likewise offer your limbs, lungs, heart, all body parts, and in this way practise emptiness.
- If all sorts of meaningless thoughts proliferate, visualise your glorious qualified lama at the five chakras in the clear central channel. Masses of light rays, subtle, fiery and projecting, pervade the channels, like guests filling a house.
- Or if your mind is weak, agitated, cannot abide and gets angry, as this is due to the winds, rub human fat or medicinal extracts at the general and wind moxibustion points.

།དེ་ལ་བསྒོམ་པའི་དུས་སུ་རྟོན་མོངས་ནི་སྲུང་འདོད་ཆགས་གཏི་མུག་གསུམ་ལ་འཕོས་ནས། བསྒོམ་གནས་སུ་མི་འདོད་པ་ལ། འབྱུང་བ་ལུས་འཁྲུག་གིས་ཚོང་པ་དང་། བདུད་ཀྱིས་ཚོང་པ་དང་གཉིས་སོ། །དེ་ལ་སློམ་ཡང་རེས་ཡང་དག་པ་ཚོང་རེས་རྣམ་རྟོག་དུ་སྤང་ན་ལུས་འཁྲུག་གི་ཉད་ཡིན། བསྒོམ་ཡེ་མི་གནས་ཞིང་ཆགས་སྤང་ཚོན་འཕོ་ན་བདུད་ཡིན། ཕྱན་འགྲོ་བས་ཕྱན་འགབ་ཀྱི་མི་བཟང་ལ་སོར་ན་གཏོན་ཡིན། རྒྱགས་འཐིབ་གཉིད་དུ་སོང་ན་ཡང་དེ་ཡིན། བསྒོམ་པ་ལ་ཞུགས་ན་གཉིད་ཆིང་མི་བསྒོམ་པར་གཉིད་མེད་ན་གཏོན་ཡིན། དེ་ལ་བདུད་ཀྱིས་མི་ཚུགས་པའི་སྲུང་བ་ནི། མཁའ་འགྲོ་ཕུགས་རྗེ་ཉེ་མའི་ཕུགས་ཀར་ཡི་དག། དེའི་ཕུགས་ཀར་རང་གི་བླ་མ། དེའི་ཕུགས་ཀར་རང་བསྒོམས་ལ་ཚ་གསུམ་གསལ་གདབ་པའི་ནང་དུ། གཏི་མུག་ཁས་ཆེན་དཔུ་མའི་ནང་ལྙ་མ་བསྒོམ། ཞེ་སྲང་གཡས་དཀར་ཡི་ངག་གྱིས་བཀག་ན། གཡོན་དམར་འདོད་ཆགས་མཁའ་འགྲོས་བཀག་རོ། །འདུན་དུ་ལྙ་མ་རྒྱད་པ་དང་བཅས་པ། ཡི་དམ་གཙོ་འཁོར་དང་བཅས་པ། མཁའ་འགྲོ་བཀའ་སྲུང་དང་བཅས་པ་ལ། ཕར་ལ་ཕྱི་ནང་གསང་བའི་མཆོད་པ་འབུལ་ཞིང་། ཆུར་ལ་ཡེ་ཤེས་བདུད་རྩིའི་ཆུ་རྒྱུན་དུ་སྤྱན་དྲངས་བས་དུག་གསུམ་སེལ་ལོ། དེ་ལྟར་བདུད་ཀྱི་བྱིན་འབྱམས་པ་མ་སེལ་བར་དུ་བྱའོ།

When at the time of meditation, the disturbing emotions of anger, desire and confusion, proliferate and you don't want to stay at the place of meditation, this is either due to a disturbance of the elements or to demons. When meditation is sometimes correct while at other times thoughts come up, it is due to illness (caused by excessive desire for) copulation. If from the start you cannot stay in meditation, and nothing but desire and anger proliferate, it is due to demons (*bdud*). If meditation deteriorates towards the end this is due to spirits (*gdon*). If one is dull and falls asleep this is also due to spirits. If you have to sleep during meditation but can't sleep outside of meditation this is due to spirits.

In order to protect against harm from demons, visualise the dakini Sun of Compassion; in her heart is the meditation deity, in the meditation deity's heart is the lama, and in the lama's heart are you. Inside the three channels you visualise (respectively): the lama in the central channel if confusion is dominant, the white right channel filled with meditation deities if anger is dominant, and the red left channel filled with dakinis if desire is dominant. In front of yourself visualise your spiritual teacher with the lineage lamas, the meditation deity with its entourage, and the dakinis and protectors. Make outer, inner and secret offerings and receive a stream of wisdom nectar until the obstacle due to the influence of demons is eliminated.

།དེ་ནས་འབྱུང་བ་ལ་རྒྱུད་འཐུམས་པ་དང་འཁྲུག །འཐུམས་གཉིས་སོ།
།རྒྱུད་འཐུམས་པ་འབྱུང་བ་རང་ལུག །ཁ་ཤས་ཆེ་བ་ཡིན། འཁྲུག་འཐུམས་འབྱུང་བ་
གཞིས་ཕྱེབས་སུ་འཁྲུག་པའོ།

།དང་པོ་འབྱུང་བ་རང་རྒྱུད་ཤ་ཁ་ཆེ་ལ་གཉན་ཁེན་གྱིས་བཙོས་ཏེ། ས་ཁ་ཆེ་བས་
ལུས་པོ་ལྗི། འགྲོ་མི་འདོད་ཤེས་པ་འབྱེ། དེ་ལ་ཁ་ཕྱོགས་གཞིས་ལ་བ་བསྐྱེ། རང་
ལུས་ལྷུ་བྱད་པ་སྐྲ་སྟོང་པར་སྐ་བའི་དཀྱིལ་འཁོར་གྱུང་ལྷུང་རེ་བ་བསམས་ལ། དེའི་
དཀྱིལ་གྱི་རྟོ་ལས་བདུད་རྗེ་དཀར་ལ་བཞིལ་བ་བབས་པར་བསམས་ཞིང་། ཐུན་ཏེ་ཕུ་
རྩ་གཅིག ཐུན་གཅིག་ཏུ་བྱས་པའི་ཐུན་བདུན་ནས་བཟེ་ཏེ་ཕུ་རྩ་གཅིག་གི་
རབ་འབྱིང་ཐ་མའི་ཆུལ་དུ་སེལ་ལོ། །མེ་ཤས་ཆེ་བ་འཆད་ཅིང་འཕོ་བ་ལ། སྤྱི་བོ་
ནས་རྩ་ཤེལ་གྱི་ཕུབ་ཁ་ལ་ཐུར་དུ་གྱུ་བ་ལས། རྒྱ་ས་ལེ་སྦྲོ་ཕྱུག་གྱང་ལྤང་ལྤང་
འབབ་པར་བསམས་ལ། ཀྲུང་སྐྲ་བཅས་སུ་ཧྲང་ཅིང་སྐྲ་བཅས་སུ་བདད། རྒྱ་ཤས་ཆེ་
བས་ལུས་གྱང་བ་སྐྱེ། ཟས་མི་འཁུན་ཅིང་པོ་བ། རྒྱ་སྐྱང་སྦྲོས་པ་ལ། ཚིག་སྐྲོར་ཡོ་
ལས་རྐྱང་བྱང་། སྐྱེ་བའི་རྩ་ལས་མི་དཔྱང་འབར་ནས། མི་ལེ་དམར་ཚུབ་ཚུབ་བསྐོང་
རྐྱང་སྐ་མེད་དུ་བཟུང་། སྐ་མེད་དུ་བདད། རྐྱང་ཤས་ཆེ་བས་འགྲོ་ལ་དགའ། ཉིང་
དེ་འཛིན་གཡེལ། ཤེས་པ་འགྲོ། དེ་ལ་སྐྱིང་ཁར་སབའི་དཀྱིལ་འཁོར་གྱུ་བའི་ལ་ཆོར་
བྱ་རིན་པོ་ཆེ་ལྡིད་ལྡིད་འདུ་བ་བཞིས་བྲར་ནས་འཕྱང་བར་བསམས་ལ། འཛམ་རྐྱང་
བཟུང་། བཀྲ་མཉེ་དང་དོང་བརྟེན། ནག་སར་བསྐོམ་མོ། དེ་ནི་འཐུང་བ་གཅིག
གིས་གཅིག་བཙོས་པའོ།

There are two types of scattering due to the elements: one type is caused by dominance (of an element) and another type is caused by disturbance (between elements). The dominant (element) that scatters is the element that is naturally stronger. Scattering due to disturbance refers to disagreement between two elements.

With regarding to the first: the element that is naturally stronger can be corrected by another element.

- If the earth element is dominant, the body is heavy, you do not want to move, and your consciousness is dull. To correct this stay in a cool place and imagine a resplendent cold moon mandala inside your body that is empty like a bellows. From a BAM in its centre descends cool white nectar. Counting twenty-one breaths as one session the best practitioner performs seven sessions to eliminate (the problem), practitioners of medium capacity perform fourteen sessions and practitioners of the lowest capacity twenty-one sessions.
- If the fire element is dominant, your meditation is weak and thoughts proliferate. To correct this, imagine that from a crystal vase that is turned upside down at your crown pure, rich, abundant, cold water descends. Inhale and exhale with sound.
- If the water element is dominant, your cold body is cold, you can't digest food, and your stomach aches, your small intestines are bloated and winds leave from the lower door. (To correct this) imagine that from RAM at your navel a heap of fire blazes with red fiery tongues. Inhale and exhale without sound.
- If the wind element is dominant, you like to move about, your concentration is lost, and your mind is fickle. To correct this, in your heart visualise a square earth mandala. Four heavy precious stones are suspended from its corners. Perform smooth breathing, take massage, stay in warm places, and meditate in dark places.

།འབྱུང་བ་བཞི་འཕྲུགས་པ་བསལ་བ་ནི། །སའི་ཁྲུང་དང་ཁྲུང་གི་ཁྲུང་གཞིས་འཕྲུགས་པ་
ལ་ནི་སྤྱང་འབའང་ཞིག་ཏུ་འབར། །ཆུ་ཁྲུང་མེ་ཁྲུང་གཞིས་འཕྲུགས་ན་འདོང་ཆགས་
ཀྱིས་སེམས་ཅན་(སེམས)ལ་སྲེད་པ་ཆེ། །ས་ཆུ་གཞིས་འཕྲུགས་ན་གཏི་སྨུག་ཏུ་འཐིབ།
དེ་ལས་ཡེ་ཤེས་རྩ་གསུམ་དུ་སྦ་བའི་ཐིག་ལེ་རྣམས་ཆུ་ཆུན་གོང་དུ་བསྟན་པ་བཞིན་
ཡང་དང་ཡང་དུ་ཁྲོ།

ཁྲིད་པ་ལ་གསུམ་སྟེ་གསང་བ་རྩ་བའི་ཁྲུང་སྦ་ཁྲིད་པ་དང་། ནང་དོན་སྦོང་གི་ཁྲུང་
ཁྲིད་པ་དང་། ཕྱི་དབང་པོ་ཡན་ལག་གི་ཁྲུང་ཁྲིད་པའོ།

With regard to elimination of disturbances between the four elements: when earth-wind and wind-wind are disturbed (not in balance) you just rage with anger. When water-wind and fire-wind are disturbed through desire, you strongly crave for beings. When earth-wind and water-wind are not in balance your confusion makes you dull. To correct this, as explained above, again and again request that the blessing of the lama enters the three wisdom channels like a stream of water.

There are three kinds of roughness: in case of secret roughness the five root winds are rough, in case of internal roughness the winds of the essential organs are rough, and in case of external roughness the winds of the senses and limbs are rough.

།དེ་ལ་དང་པོ་སྟེང་ཁའི་རླུང་སྒོག་འཛིན་དྲེད་པས། སྟེང་རླུང་བསྐྱོ་(སྐྱོ་)འབོགས་སུ་
འགྱུར། དེ་ལ་སྟེང་ཁའི་ཏུཾ་ལ་ཤེས་པ་གཏད་ལ་ཀང་པ་གཉིས་རྒྱ་གྲམ་གྱི་སྐྱིལ་ཀྲུང་
བཙས་ནས་གན་རྒྱལ་དུ་འདུག་སྟེ། ལག་པའི་ཀང་མཐེབ་ལ་འཇུས་ལ་རླུང་ཤུང་
ཟད་མནན་ཞིང་སྐྲ་ར་ར་སྐྱོར་ཕྱུན་གཉིས་གསུམ་གྱིས་སོས་སོ། །མགྲིན་པའི་གྱེན་རྒྱུ་
དྲེད་པས་རླུགས་པའམ་གྱི་འགག་ཏུ་འགྱུར། དེ་ལ་སྐྱིལ་ཀྲུང་བཙས་ནས་ན་བ་
གཉིས་ནས་ཡར་འཐེན་མར་དྲག་པོ་བཙབ་པར་བྱའོ། །ཡང་ན་གོས་ཕུར་དུ་གཞུག
ལ་གཡུག་པས་འཕལ་དུ་སྐྱོན་སེལ་ལོ། །ཁྲབ་ཏེད་དྲེད་པས་ཚོགས་ཐམས་ཅད་ན་བ
ལ། དྲག་ཤུལ་གྱི་མཚོང་རྒྱག་ཉིད་ཀྱིས་སེལ་ལོ། །ཕྱེ་བའི་མེ་མཉམ་དྲེད་པ་ལ། སྦོས་
དང་མེ་ཞུ་ཕོ་བ་སྐྲེགས་པ་འབྱུང་། དེ་ལ་སྐྱིལ་ཀྲུང་བཙས་པའི་ནང་དུ་ལག་པ
གཉིས་བཏོན་ལ། གཏུད་དུ་འདོར་ཞིང་མགོ་བོ་ཕྱར་དུ་འཆུང་ལ་རྒྱུ་སྨུག་པ་དང་
སྐྱིག་བུ་བཏོན་པས་སེལ་ལོ། ཕྱར་སེལ་དྲེད་པས་ཟུག་བསྐྱེད་དེ་རྒྱུ་བསྒམས་པ་ལ།
ཚིག་ཕྱུར་བྱས་ཁེང་མཚོང་རྒྱག་དང་། གཟུང་སྟེ་བར་དུ་མཉེ་བསྒྱུབ་བྱ། དེས་ནི་རྩ
བའི་རླུང་ལྔ་དྲེད་པ་བསལ་བའོ།

As to the first:

- When the life-supporting wind at the heart is rough, you will have heart-wind and become crazy. To cure this, focus the mind on a HUM in the heart, lie on your back with the two legs in cross-legged position like crossed sceptres, the hands holding the big toes, press the wind slightly, and turn around two or three times.
- When the upward voiding wind at the throat is rough you will be mute or your throat will be blocked. To correct this, sit in cross-legged position and strongly pull the ears upward and downward[42]. Alternatively, this problem will be eliminated instantly when you stay in a cloth that is raised up and tossed about.
- When the all-pervading wind is rough all your joints hurt. To correct this, run and make fierce jumps.
- When the fire-equalising wind at the navel is rough, you are bloated, can't digest, and your stomach belches. To correct this, sit in cross-legged position, put the two hands inside (the legs), hang the head downward, vomit and belch.
- When the downward-clearing wind is rough this causes pain, and faeces and urine are blocked. To eliminate this stay in the *rishi* position, jump and run, and massage the perineum.

This is the way to eliminate roughness of the five root winds.

---

42   With both hands alternately pulling one side upward and the other side downward.

།ནང་དོན་སྟིང་ལྷ་ལ་རྐྱང་རང་གནས་སུ་མ་འཆུན་པས་དེང་པ་བསལ་བ་ནི། སྟིང་
དང་རོ་སྐྱོད་གཟེར་ཞིང་ན། ཕྱི་རོལ་དུ་ཕོ་གདོན་འབབ་ཞིག་གདོན། འདུ་བ་ཁྲག
དང་མཐིས་པ་འཕུར། ཉོན་མོངས་པ་ནེ་སྤུང་རྒྱས། ཅིང་འཛིན་སྐྱོང་པ་ཟར་དུ་མི་
སྟེར། དེ་ལ་སྟིང་ཁར་རྒྱ་རྩུའི་དགྱེར་འཁོར་དུ་ཡི་དགས་བསྐྱེད། བསྐལ་པ་གསུམ་སྟོམ་
པས་སྤྱངས། སྟོང་ཉིད་ལ་གཞིར་བཞག སྟར་འདོན་གྱིས་ཕྱིར་འཐྲེན། དེ་འདའི་ཕུན་
རེ་ལ་ནི་ཤུ་རྩ་གཅིག་བྲས་པས། རབ་ཕྱུན་གཅིག་འཐིང་ལ་བདུན། ཐ་མ་བཅུ
གསུམ་ཆུན་ཅད་ཀྱིས་གྲོལ་ལོ། །བསྐལ་པ་གསུམ་གྱི་རོ་ལ་མེ་སྦྱར་བས་བཟེར། མི
ལས་རྒྱ་བབས་པས་བཀྱུག ཡོ་ལས་རྐྱང་བྱུང་བས་བ་སྦྱུའི་བུ་གར་ཕྱིར་སྟོན་དམར་
བྱུན་བྱུན་སྟར་ཞིང་འདོན་པའོ། །སྟོང་ར་ནེ་དེ་དེ་རྗེས་སྟོང་པ་ཞིང་གར་མི་བདེ་སར་
བསྒོམ་པའོ།

།གཏུམ་མོ་བསྒོམ་ལོག མགོ་ན་ཞིང་སྟེ། ནད་བད་ཀན་གྱིས་རྒྱས། གདོན་ས་བདག་
གྲུ་གཞན་གདོན། གཏེ་སྨུག་སྨུན་པས་མཐའབ་རྒྱས། ཉམས་གསལ་བ་ཟར་དུ་མི་སྟེར།
དེ་ལ་སྒྲད་པ་དང་ཁང་གི་རྣ་གདན་ལ་ན་ཟ་མ་བསྒོམ་ཞིང་བསྐལ་པ་སྟར་འདོན་སྟོང་
ར་རྐྱང་དང་བཅས་པ་བྱའོ།

།འདོད་ཆགས་ཤས་ཆེ་བའི་སྐྱེས་བུ་དེ། མགལ་ནད་དང་གྲང་བ་ཅན་དུ་འོང་། མོ
གདོན་རིགས་སུ་གྱུར་པས་ཉམས་ལེན། ཅིང་དེ་འཛིན་བདེ་ཆེན་གྱི་རོ་མི་སྐྱོང་། དེ
ལ་སྟེ་འོག་ཏུ་ནི་མའི་དགྱིལ་འཁོར་ལ་མཁའ་འགྲོ་མ་ཁྲོ་རྒྱ་ཁོལ་མ་ལྷ་བུའི་སྐུ
བསྒོམ། བསྐལ་པ་སྟར་འདོན་སྟོང་ར་རྐྱང་དང་བཅས་པས་སེལ་ལོ།
།དེ་ལྟར་ཉོན་མོངས་པ་དུག་གསུམ་དུ་ནད་གདོན་བསྟས་པ་དེ་བཞིན་དུ། ནད་དོན་
སྟོད་གང་ལ་ཡང་དེས་འཇེས་སོ།

Internally when the winds do not stay in their natural place in the essential organs and have become rough, eliminate (the problem) as follows:

- When the heart and upper part of the body are painful and ill, externally interferences come from male spirits only, blood pressure and bile rise up, the disturbing emotion of anger increases, and (the experience of) emptiness does not arise through contemplation, correct this by imagining the meditation deity in the heart on top of a mandala of sun and moon. Purify with the radiation (of the elements) of the three eons. Settle in emptiness. Expel the wind (breath out) upward. Doing this, twenty-one times those of best capacity will liberate (the problem) within one session, those of middling capacity within seven sessions and those of lowest capacity within thirteen sessions. As regards the elements of (the end of an) eon: from RAM comes fire that burns, from MAM descends water that washes, and from YAM arises wind that expels a purple coloured vapour from the pores. As to the hollow interior: thereafter meditate that the place that is uncomfortable is (hollow) emptiness.
- When you have meditated on inner fire in the wrong way, your head will hurt and feel heavy, you will go crazy due to phlegm illness, interferences will come from earth spirits, *nagas* or rock spirits (*gnyan*), the darkness of confusion will be total, and the experience of clarity will not come. Correct this by meditating the spiritual master on a moon seat in the shell-house in the brain, expel with the three (elements) of an eon, and (meditate) hollow emptiness. Combine this with breathing.
- Beings for whom desire is dominant have illness of the kidneys and are cold, have interferences from the class of female spirits, and do not experience the taste of great bliss of contemplation. Correct this by meditating on a dakini with a body of molten bronze on a sun mandala below the navel, expel with the three (elements) of an eon, and (meditate) hollow emptiness. Combine this with breathing.

This is how the three poisons of the disturbing emotions (correspond) with illness and spirits. The other essential organs are similar.

ཁྱི་དབང་པོ་ཡན་ལག་གི་རྐྱང་དྲེད་བསལ་བ་ནི། སྟེང་ནང་དུ་རྒྱ་གྲང་བླུག་པ་འང་
ཞིང་སེམས་མི་བདེ་ན། །སྒོག་རྩ་འགག་པ་ཡིན་པས་སྟེང་ལ་གོང་བཞིན་ཡི་དགས་
བསྒོམ། དང་ལ་འཚོང་བ་འདུ་ན་སྒྲོ་སྟེང་ལ་བླ་མ་བསྒོམ་ཞིང་སྐྱེ་ཐར་གཅུ་ཆུང་
གཅུ་བྱ། སྐྱེ་དང་ལ་སྒོག་རྒྱལ་པ་སེལ་ལོ། །ཤུ་བྲང་ན་ན་ཡེ་ཤེས་ཀྱི་འཁོར་ལོ་རྩེན་པོ་
ལ་མཁའ་འགྲོ་མ་བཞུགས་པས། འོད་ཟེར་སྒྲོ་ཞིང་བསྒོར་བས་ནད་རྣམས་རེག
རེག་སྲེག་པར་བསམ། ཀེད་པ་ན་འབའམ་སྐྱུར་པར་སོང་བ་ལ། ཀེད་པ་ཐན་ཆུན་དུ་
སྐྱལ་ཞིང་རྐྱང་བབྱུང་བས་མགྲིན་པ་བསྐམ་མོ། །ཕྱི་པོ་ན་ན་སྦྱིན་མཚམས་ཡན་ཆད་
བྲེགས་ནས་སྟོང་སང་ངེ་བསྒོམ། མགོ་གཞིགས་ན་ན་ལ་ནང་ནས་ཡེ་ཤེས་འབོར་
པོས་བྲེག་པ་དང་། ཕྱི་ནས་བླ་མའི་ཞུན་ཁུས་བཞིག་པར་བསམ་མོ། །མིག་ན་བ་ལ་
ནམ་མཁའི་མཐོངས་ཕྱི་བ་ལ་མིག་བར་སྐྲང་ལ་སྐར་ཆེན་བཞིན་བསྒོམ་པ་དང་།
དངོས་པོའི་གནས་བསྒྱུར་བ་མིག་སྟོང་པ་ཉིད་དུ་བསྒོམ་པ་དང་། ཡུལ་གྱི་སྣང་བ་
བསྒྱུར་བ་མིག་ལྷ་མར་བསམ་མོ། །རྣ་བ་གཟེར་བ་ལ། །རང་གི་ལྡི་ཆུ་བར་པ་བླུག་ལ་
བལ་གྱིས་བཙང་། རྐྱང་བབྱུང་ཞིང་བཏུང་བ་རྣ་བར་སོང་བར་བསམས་ལ་དུས་
གཅིག་བཏང་ངོ་། །འོན་པ་ལ་ཡེ་ཤེས་དཔར་ཐབ་དུ་དཔར་འགྲོ་ཆུལ་འགྲོ་བྱེད་པ་
དང་། བླ་མའི་བདུད་རྩི་ན་ར་ར་བབས་པ་རེས་ཚོས་བྱ། སྣ་ན་བ་དང་མཆུལ་པ་
འགག་པ་ལ་རྐྱང་བབྱུང་ཞིང་སྐྱེ་ཐར་ཆུན་དུ་གཅུ་བའོ།

Externally when the winds of the senses and limbs become rough eliminate (the problem) as follows:

- When you feel as if cold water is poured into your heart and your mind is uncomfortable, as this is due to blockage of the life force channel, meditate on the meditation deity in the heart like above.
- When you lack appetite (imagine) the spiritual master in the lungs and heart, and turn the neck back and forth. This eliminates swelling in the throat and mouth.
- When the upper chest is painful (meditate on) a dakini that stays on a sharp wisdom wheel and radiates swirling light rays that burn all illness.
- When the waist is painful and you are bent down, move the waist to and fro while you hold the breath and close the throat.
- When the crown is painful, meditate that your head is cut off at the brows and above it is completely emptiness.
- When the side of the head is painful, imagine that a wisdom-wheel cuts the head from the inside and it is burnt by hot liquid coming from the spiritual master from the outside.
- When the eyes are painful, meditate that the eyes are big stars in the atmosphere of vast open space, meditate the eyes are (hollow) emptiness, and consider the eyes to be the spiritual teacher.
- When the ears are painful, fill a cup with the middle part of your own urine (by pouring it through) pure wool, hold the breath while you take it in one go considering it goes to the ears.
- When you are deaf, alternate imagining a wisdom HA going back and forth, and nectar flowing down from the spiritual teacher.
- When your nose is painful and blocked, hold your breath and turn the neck.

།མཚུལ་ཁུང་ན་ཞིང་འགག་པ་ལ། ལག་པ་གཉིས་འཐུག་མགོ་ལ་འཇུས་ལ་རོ་སྟོང་
གཡས་གཅུ་གཡོན་གཅུ་བྱའོ། །བྲེ་བ་ན་བ་ལ་ཁྲི་གཅུ་ངག་བསུམ་ཞིན་རྐྱང་བབུང་
ངོ་། །བྲེ་བ་འགག་པ་ལ། མཆན་གཞུང་ཆིག་འདི་རྣམས་བརྟེན་འགྱུར་དུ་གསལ།)
ཆུ་གི་འཕྲོ་འདུས་ཡི་དམ་དང་དུས་མཉམ་དུ་བྱའོ། །སོ་ན་བ་ལ་རྐྱང་དང་དཀྱིལ་ག
པ་མེག་དང་མཐུན་པར་བྱའོ། །སྲིང་འཕར་བ་ལ་གསེར་གྱི་མཆོང་རྟེན་གྱིས་མནན་
པར་བསྐོས། །སྲིང་ན་བ་ལ་ཡེ་ཤེས་བསྲུང་བྱུས་གཟེར་བས་ནད་བཏོན་པར་བསམ།
སྐྲ་བ་(ཱ)ཌོ་ལ་བྱེད་པ་ལ་གཏོན་ཡིན་ན། སྦྲེལ་ཆེན་པོའི་སྦྲུ་རྩེ་མེག་གིས་གང་བ
གཅིག་གི་ནང་དུ་རང་ཡི་དམ་དུ་བསམས་ལ་ཤལ་ལོ། །འབྱུལ་པ་ཆེན་བྱང་རྒྱབ་ཀྱི
ཕོད་པ་ལ་སྦྱོར་སྦྱབ་མེད་གཅིག་ཏུ་རང་རྒྱུད་པར་བསམ། གཤིས་འབྱུལ་ལ་རང་
སེམས་ཉི་མའི་སྐེང་དུ་ཨ་ལ་ཤེས་པ་གཏད་དོ།

།བྱིར་གསང་སྔགས་ཀྱི་ལུགས་ཀྱི་གང་ལ་ཡང་རྩ་དྲུ་མ་ནས། འབྲོར་ལོ་ལྩ་ལ་སྟེ
བའི་མེ་རྒྱན་རེ་བསྲིང་རེ་བསྲིང་བྱས་པས་ནད་གཏོན་བསྒེག་པར་བསམ་མོ།
།སྤར་སྤར་ཉིན་རེར་ཐུན་བཞི་རེ་སྦྲང་བཞིན་ཐུན་མཐར་རྣམས་སུ་འགྲེལ་ལས
བྱང་བའི་གེགས་སེལ་དང་། པོགས་འདོན་རྣམས་རིམ་བཞིན་བསྐྱན་ཞིང་སྦྲང་པའོ

- When the nostrils are painful and blocked, hold the upper arms and turn left and right.
- When the throat is painful, spread and absorb (light) from and HUM while at the same time (visualising) the meditation deity. (When the throat is painful hold the wind, restrain the voice, and turn the neck. When the throat is blocked (what to do) is clarified in the collection of commentaries (*bka'-brten*))
- When your teeth are painful, bring the wind and object of focus in line with the eyes.
- When the heart palpitates, meditate that a golden stupa presses down on it.
- When your heart is painful, imagine that the pain of wisdom that is like a boring awl digs out the illness.
- When your vital force (*bla*) dissipates, if it is due to (interference of) spirits, fall asleep while you imagine that the hairs of a big monkey fill the eyes, and in between them is the meditation deity.
- When you are heavily deluded, imagine you are inside a seamless skull of enlightenment.
- When you are naturally confused, focus on your mind in the form of an A on top of a sun.

In general in all types of tantric teaching, you imagine that inside the central channel in the centre of the five chakra-wheels fire continuously burns illnesses and spirits. As before practice four sessions a day and at the end of each session practice the elimination of obstacles and enhancement.

།ཁ་མའི་ཉེན་ལྟ་ལ་རྗེ་སྤར་འགྲེལ་ལས་གསལ་བཞིན་གེགས་སེལ་དང་ཕོགས་
འདོན་རྣམས་སྦྱང་བར་བྱ། དགོས་དུས་ལག་ལེན་ཐོབ་པར་བྱེད།

ཆུ་རས་སོགས་བྱེད་པར་འདོད་ན་དུས་ཀྱི་ཐ་མ་འདིར་ཁྲིད་གཞན་ནས་བྱུང་
བཞིན་བྱེད། འདིར་ཆུད་འགྲེལ་རྣམས་སུ་མ་གསལ་བས་བྲར་བཀོད་མ་བྱས། ཨ་
སྨྲ་རྫོགས་གསུམ་སོགས་ཀྱི་གེགས་སེལ་དང་འཕུལ་འཁོར་སྦྱང་བར་འདོད་ན་
རང་རང་གི་གཞུང་དང་བསྟན་ནས་ཕྱག་ལེན་མཛོད།

The last five days you can practise the elimination of obstacles and enhancement, as they are explained in the commentary. In this way you will know how to do them when you need them.

If at the end (of the retreat) you wish to dry cotton clothes etc. you can do so as described in other manuals. Because these (type of practice) are not explained in the (Mother) tantra and its commentary I have not commented. If you wish to practice the elimination of obstacles and magical movements of the Atri, Zhang Zhung Nyen Gyu or Dzogchen, you can practice them according to these texts.

།ལྷགས་དོན་ཐིས་པ་འགགས་ཡེ་རྱུར་རྒྱན་རྩུལ།།

།མ་རྱུད་འགྲེལ་བའི་དགོངས་དོན་ལག་ལེན་ཆེ།།

།རྩ་རྩུང་ཐིག་ལེ་སྦྱང་བའི་རྩུལ་འདི་ནི།།

།ལྷགས་ལམ་རིམ་གཉིས་བསྒྲུབ་པའི་ཐབས་ཀྱི་གཙོ།།

།འདི་སྣར་དགོས་པ་མཚོང་བའི་བཤེས་གཉེན་ཚོས།།

།སྐྱལ་བར་མཛད་པ་ཡར་བར་མ་དོར་ནས།།

།འབྱུང་ཕུང་ནད་ཀྱིས་བཟུང་ཡང་བསྟན་ལ་བསམ།།

།ཚོངས་པའི་ཚོགས་རྣམས་བཀགས་ནིང་དགེ་བ་སྦྲོ།།

།བསྟན་འཛིན་རྣམ་དག་གིས་ཐིས།།

I have written (this manual) how to practice with channels, wind and *tigles,*
as an appendix to my previous writings on the meaning of mantra.
Its purpose is to practice in accordance with the commentary to the Mother Tantra.
It is the main practice method of the two stages of the path of mantra.

So as to not forsake the request of the *geshes,*
who have seen this to be necessary,
even though I am affected by physical illness, I aspire to explain this.
I confess all errors and dedicate the virtue.

Written by Tendzin Namdhak